A Student's Guide to NATIVE AMERICAN Genealogy

Oryx American Family Tree Series

A Student's Guide to NATIVE AMERICAN Genealogy

By E. Barrie Kavasch

Oryx Press
1996

To All Children
You Are Our Future!

My warm gratitude to Roger Rosen and the entire Rosen
Publishing Group for determination, courage, and vision in
bringing this book, and series, to life! Much appreciation to
my good friends at the American Indian College Fund and
the Institute for American Indian Studies. My respect and
admiration to all of the Native American voices echoing
throughout time, and within the pages of this little book.
Thank you!

Finally, my love to my own dear family. This could not
have been possible without you all. May we walk in
harmony!

Copyright 1996 by The Rosen Publishing Group, Inc.
Published in 1996 by The Oryx Press
4041 North Central at Indian School Road
Phoenix, Arizona 85012-3397

Printed and bound in the United States of America

⊗ The paper used in this publication meets the minimum requirements
of American National Standard for Information Science—Permanence of
Paper for Printed Library Materials, ANSI Z39.48, 1984.
Library of Congress Cataloging-in-Publication Data
Kavasch, E. Barrie.
    A student's guide to Native American genealogy / by E. Barrie
Kavasch.
        p.   cm. — (Oryx American family tree)
    Includes bibliographical references and index.
    ISBN 0-89774-975-8
        1. Indians North America—Genealogy—Handbooks, manuals,
etc.   2. Indians of North America—Genealogy—Bibliography.
I. Title.   II. Series: Oryx American family tree.
E98.G44K39   1996
929'.1'08997—dc20   96-10196
                                                            CIP

Contents

Chapter 1
Grandmother Spider's Tangled Web

"We need to remember the contributions our forefathers found here and from which they borrowed liberally. . . . Collectively their history is our history and should be part of our shared and remembered heritage."
—President John Fitzgerald Kennedy in the introduction to *The American Heritage Book of Indians* by William Brandon

Grandmother Spider is significant in understanding the creation story of many Native American peoples. According to early Cherokee beliefs, she helped the first people to get the sun and fire to cook their food and keep them warm. Some Navajo beliefs say that Grandmother Spider weaves the vital threads of life in beautiful, colorful patterns like those we see in Navajo rugs and blankets. Many Native American people say that Grandmother Spider weaves us all together.

You may see some interesting parallels with Grandmother Spider as you trace your history back generations to find where your family threads touch other family threads and interweave themselves. Genealogy is a personal history; a study of your ancestry and the details of how your family descends from earlier kinfolk. Tracking this valuable information back through time is a little like weaving a beautiful rug or tapestry of your own.

The major focus of this book is on Native Americans in the territorial United States, but some of the information will also be useful for readers with Canadian, Alaskan, Hawaiian, Mexican, Central American, and South American roots. Many of these resources will help to point you in the right direction, so you can dig deeper into your family's

This Navajo weaver in the Southwest adds the various colored wool threads to complete her geometric design. Navajo rugs are masterpieces; some patterns have distinctive names and legends associated with them, and can take a year or more to weave. Reconstructing your family history is like weaving a beautiful rug of your own.

origins. In Bridgeport, New York City, Boston, Seattle, or Los Angeles, our growing native populations are as likely to include Aleut, Tlingit, Maya, Tarahumara, Taino, Navajo, Chippewa, Winnebago, Cherokee, and Hopi families as they are to include Pequot, Mohegan, Shinnecock, Wampanoag, Mohawk, Seneca, Cayuga, Oneida, Onondaga, and Tuscarora families.

Questions of Identity

Not all native peoples consider themselves to be North American Indians, so we use this historic term along with the term Native Americans, which more inclusively embraces Native peoples. Aleut, Inuit, Inupiat, Yup'ik, G'wichin, and other northern groups are not considered "Indians" and are more closely related to their Siberian counterparts. Also, Hawaiian Islanders are not considered "Indians," as they are more closely related to their Polynesian origins. Yet, you might ask: Aren't we all "Native Americans" if we were born here? Yes, we are. In this book, however, as in numerous other scholarly and government sources, the term Native Americans signifies "indigenous peoples"—those whose ancestors originated in North America. Confused? I hope not. These are just the verbal tools of our times.

The Native American Past

Native American peoples have an ancient history on the North American continent. Native American culture has been continually evolving for longer than we may know. This richly detailed, often mysterious past continues to inform our present and our future with extraordinary monuments, ceremonial sites, earthworks, temples, and a diverse range of artifacts created by ancient hands and minds. This past is a valuable part of American and Canadian history. Indeed, all of North America and the Western Hemisphere share much of this history.

Native Americans have overcome remarkable odds. In the past 500 years, Native Americans have endured displacement from their lands and destruction of their ways of life. The European colonization and settlement of North America caused major changes among these diverse native peoples whom settlers called "Indians." During colonial days the Continental Congress appointed the first Indian commissioners, including Patrick Henry and Benjamin Franklin, to oversee trade, land deals, and military concerns involving Native Americans. The U.S. government later attempted to appropriate Native American lands in the eastern United States and move whole tribal populations to "new" lands in Indian Territory in the West. This territory was carved from the Louisiana Purchase of 1803, in which the U.S. government acquired the formerly Spanish region of Louisiana from France.

Chiefs of the Flathead tribe gathered at the Flathead Indian Reservation in Missoula, Montana, in 1921 and posed against the scenic backdrop of the Bitterroot Mountains. Like many other Native American tribes, the Flatheads were forced by white settlers to abandon their ancestral land in the second half of the nineteenth century and were settled with other tribes on a reservation.

The non-Indian population of North America grew, and conflicts between settlers and Native Americans continued to flare up around the country, although in countless areas peaceful coexistence was the norm. Land purchases and economic developments led to further disruptions in Native American life. The land-reliant Native economies, based upon reciprocity of exchange for foods, medicines, and spiritual sustenance, were uprooted.

Native American lands in the West soon became as coveted as the eastern lands had been. United States government policies concerning Native Americans were shaped largely with military force. These periods during the nineteenth century were known as the Indian Wars. More than a century of treaty-making, creating Native American reservations and trust lands, was followed by repeated government attempts to break up tribal land holdings. The ever-changing aims of the U.S. government created greater dilemmas in trying to resolve old problems between indigenous Americans and the descendants of European settlers.

The Indian Reorganization Act of 1934 provided for restoration of tribal governments and launched new policies of federal technical and financial aid to tribal groups. The Bureau of Indian Affairs was granted control over more than 50 million acres of Native American lands. Although the act is still in effect today, some Native Americans disagree with its goals, believing that its aim is to gradually assimilate Native Americans into American society.

Native Americans Today

More than 500 federally recognized tribes in the United States include more than 200 Alaskan Native village groups. Additionally, there are more than 600 Native Canadian Indian reserves and tribes.

Native peoples today often balance traditional values with modern life. Many embrace their timeless heritage and follow traditional pathways of herbalism, healing, farming, hunting, artistry, and fine craftwork. As cooks, weavers, cowboys, rodeo riders, poets, artists, playwrights, and musicians, they ply their traditional crafts. My grandmothers, aunts, and other relatives were marvelous seamstresses. They made the family's clothes and quilts, and when these wore thin they rolled and braided the spent fabrics into braided rugs—some of which are in a museum today. My mother can still "read" these rugs and point out the different family members' outfits from which they were made. Quilt patterns and braided rugs are unique "languages" and "records" of period history and family thriftiness.

Current U.S. census figures show that Native populations have been increasing more than 70 percent per decade since 1960, and more than 2 million Native Americans (American Indians, Aleut, Inuit, and Hawaiian Islanders) live in the United States today. Alaska has more than 75,000 Aleut and Inuit. California tops all states with 250,000 Native Americans, followed by Oklahoma and Arizona, each with 200,000, and New Mexico with 150,000. The 1990 census,

Native Americans participate in all sectors of American life, while often simultaneously embracing aspects of their traditional cultures and expressing their pride in their heritage. Above, Ramon Orona Bahad, an Apache, listens to opening statements at the Parliament of the World's Religions in Chicago in 1993.

along with Bureau of Indian Affairs figures, indicate that about 800,000 Native Americans live on or near reservations, while another 1.2 million Native Americans live in or near cities and other areas across the United States. Many authorities believe these figures underestimate the true population numbers.

Native Americans today live every conceivable lifestyle and work at every kind of job, from serving in the U.S. Congress to "walking high steel" in skyscraper construction. Native American men and women are tribal, corporate, and academic leaders, lawyers, doctors, research scientists, artists, writers, activists, actors, and musicians. Tribal leaders in many communities have achieved great success and continue to work for greater balance and economic opportunities for their people. Bright success stories are realized on many reservations, whereas others struggle with poverty and social problems, legacies of the breakdown of traditional lifestyles.

Native Americans distinguish themselves, both on and off reservations, in every region of this country. Sources of power and prestige within Native American communities vary from tribe to tribe, yet often center around jobs in tribal government, health care, and education. Tribal senior citizens centers and youth centers are bright points on most reservations, where the elders are often requested to teach traditional ways. Tribal libraries and museums on some reservations offer a broad range of learning opportunities, including computer programming. Tribal librarian, tribal historian, and Native ethnohistorian are prestigious and demanding jobs today. Narragansett Tribal Historian and Medicine Woman Dr. Ella Thomas Sekatau (in Kenyon, Rhode Island), one of my early teachers, helped me with parts of this book, along with my good friend, Schaghticoke Historian, and Master Storyteller Trudie Lamb Richmond in Kent, Connecticut, who is assistant director of the Institute for American Indian Studies in Washington, Connecticut. Each of these dynamic Algonquian Elders (*Elders* is a term of honor and distinction and does not imply elderly) has been an educator and leader most of her life. From the

Florida Seminole and Miccosukee Reservations to the Makah Reservation on the Olympic Peninsula on Washington State's rugged Pacific Coast, modern jobs and training mingle with respected traditional lifeways and jobs of basket-weaving, sewing, doll-making, and carving.

Many highly acclaimed Native American authors have enriched the broad field of literature. For example, N. Scott Momaday, noted Kiowa-Cherokee author/poet, received the Pulitzer prize (1969) for his novel *House Made of Dawn* (1968), which details the tumultuous life of a mixed-blood American Indian man who is a World War II veteran. Similar themes are echoed in his 1989 novel, *The Ancient Child*, about a middle-aged artist who finds healing through immersion in his tribal traditions. The fine novel *Winter in the Blood* (1975) by the noted Blackfeet-Gros Ventre writer James Welch follows a man's search for the truth about his family background, and in *The Death of Jim Loney* (1979) and *Indian Lawyer* (1990) Welch continues to deal poignantly with the themes of American Indian searches for identity. Both are resonant with Blackfeet history and lifeways. Welch's historical novel *Fools Crow* (1986) vividly details the hardships faced by Blackfeet in Montana during the 1870s with the encroachment of white settlements on their territory.

Gifted Laguna Pueblo writer Leslie Marmon Silko uses the energies of tribal storytelling in her powerful novel *Ceremony* (1977) about a mixed-blood Indian World War II veteran reunited with his tribe. Her books *Storyteller* (1981), a rich collection of short stories and poetry, and *Almanac of the Dead* (1991) describe the ritual quests for identity and balance among people of the Americas. Paula Gunn Allen, a Laguna-Sioux writer, offers a feminist perspective on these themes in *The Woman Who Owned the Shadows* (1983). Oral histories and traditions continue to inspire American Indian literature, as Louise Erdrich, who is of Ojibway (Chippewa) descent, shows us in her popular novel *Love Medicine* (1984), which explores the interrelationships between generations of Chippewa people in North Dakota. She contin-

A California Indian woman in Humboldt County, California (1933), displays her woven baskets. Basket-weaving, pottery-making, storytelling, art, and herbalism are among the many Native American traditions still practiced today.

ues these threads and characters through her subsequent novels *Beet Queen* (1986) and *Tracks* (1988). Her husband, Michael Dorris, of Modoc descent, is noted for many works, including his novel set on a Montana reservation, *A Yellow Raft on Blue Water* (1987), dealing with three generations of mixed-blood women torn by secrets and hardships, barely mended by kinship. Together this talented husband and wife team continue to accomplish much, and in 1991 they coauthored *The Crown of Columbus*, a humorous account of the adventures of an anthropologist of mixed blood coping with a series of crises. The novel reflects upon our nation's quincentenary, marking the 500 years since America was "discovered." Perhaps it is not surprising that so much of Native American prose—in every conceivable form—deals with the realities of origins, birthrights, bloodlines, and generations of descent. These aspects of ourselves and our "fit" within families seem to absorb us at every level of our consciousness. This may explain your own interest in family history.

A growing number of Americans are recognizing that they have Native American ancestry, and there is increasing pride in a heritage that was once borne with shame and secrecy, and worse, has long been badly treated. The Jim Crow policy of discriminating against African Americans and Indians in areas such as education, transportation, and employment, caused untold hardships for many families of color for centuries. Jim Crowism (Jim Crow was a character in an old minstrel-show song in the mid-1800s) still haunts some people of Native descent, who denied their heritage so they could go to white schools and other segregated institutions.

Today, many school children take pride in their American Indian heritage—whether they are dark-skinned, curly-haired, blond, or blue-eyed. Sometimes they know their specific ancestry; sometimes they have only heard about an Indian relative.

Researching your Native American ancestry will take you many places, perhaps on many exciting journeys, and more deeply into your own unique origins. Honor and enjoy the journey.

Resources

STARTING YOUR EXPLORATION

Ancona, George. *POWWOW*. New York: Harcourt Brace Jovanovich, 1993.

These award-winning photographs and fine text follow the Crow Fair in Montana, the largest powwow held in the United States. Illustrated with glorious, energy-filled shots—especially of Indian children and young adults.

Braine, Susan. *Drumbeat . . . Heartbeat: A Celebration of the Powwow*. We Are Still Here Series: Native Americans Today. Minneapolis: Lerner Publications, 1995.

A talented Assiniboine writer and photographer brings the colorful traditions of powwow to sensitive new light, emphasizing the Northern Plains styles of celebration and the universal language of powwow.

Carlson, Laurie. *More than Moccasins: A Kid's Activity Guide to Traditional North American Indian Life*. Chicago: Chicago Review Press, 1994.

This is a fun-filled activity book for kids to learn more about Native American lifeways.

Ferris, Jeri. *Native American Doctor: The Story of Susan La Flesche Picotte*. Minneapolis: Lerner Publications, Carolrhoda Books, 1991.

A notable book for young readers on the life of a respected Omaha doctor who rose to national prominence as a passionate Native American rights activist who lectured audiences about years of broken treaties and thefts of Indian lands.

Green, Rayna. *Women in American Indian Society.* **New York: Chelsea House, 1992.**

A look at the role of women in Native American society throughout history. Illustrated.

Hirschfelder, Arlene B., and Singer, Beverly R., eds. *Rising Voices: Writings of Young Native Americans.* **New York: Scribner, 1992.**

Presents writings from young Native Americans describing their experiences with and views on family, ritual and ceremony, education, and other topics.

Josephy, Alvin M., Jr. *500 Nations: An Illustrated History of North American Indians.* **New York: Alfred A. Knopf, 1994.**

This is a major new work, extensively illustrated, based on a documentary film by Pathways Productions.

Kavasch, E. Barrie. *EarthMaker's Lodge: Native American Folklore, Activities, and Foods.* **Peterborough, NH: Cobblestone Publishing, 1994.**

Award-winning guide "from ancient civilizations to contemporary times" sharing the diverse beliefs, traditions, and interrelationships of Native American tribes, along with many stories and projects—including a brief activity of searching for your Native American roots.

———. *Enduring Harvests: Native American Foods and Festivals for Every Season.* **Old Saybrook, CT: Globe Pequot Publishing, 1995.**

Carefully examines a typical year in contemporary North America, sharing more than 150 recipes, describing more than seventy Native American events, and featuring contributions from many different Native peoples, along with details of historic importance.

———. *Herbal Traditions: Medicinal Plants in American Indian Life.* **Washington, DC: Smithsonian Insti-**

tution-SITES (Smithsonian Institution Traveling Exhibition Service), 1984.

Detailed study of sixteen selected native plants, written and illustrated by the author, accompanying the national touring exhibition "Native Harvests: Plants in American Indian Life."

————. *Native Harvests: Recipes and Botanicals of the American Indians*. New York: Random House/Vintage Books, 1979.

A broad look at American Indian ethnobotany, especially regional, seasonal foods. Highlights wild edibles such as mushrooms, as well as medicines, cosmetics, chewing gum, and smoking mixtures derived from plants. Botanical illustrations by the author. One of the first books in the field of ethnobotany.

King, Sandra. *Shannon: An Obijway Dancer*. We Are Still Here Series: Native Americans Today. Minneapolis: Lerner Publications, 1993.

A personal look at a talented young powwow dancer on a fascinating path of discovery.

Roberts, Chris. *Powwow Country*. Helena, MT: American & World Geographic Publishing, 1992.

A bright celebration of the dance, written by a dancer, honoring a unique "way of life and emblem of a proud culture."

Roessel, Monty. *Kinaalda: A Navajo Girl Grows Up*. Minneapolis: Lerner Publications, 1993.

This Navajo author and photographer has sensitively documented the rich fabric of contemporary Navajo life. Kinaalda is the traditional Navajo ceremony welcoming a young girl into puberty, based on the ancient honoring ceremony for "Changing Woman, the First Woman."

Seymour, Tryntje Van Ness. *When the Rainbow Touches Down: The Artists and Stories Behind the Apache, Navajo, Rio Grande Pueblo, and Hopi Paintings in the William and Leslie Van Ness Denman Collection.* **Seattle: University of Washington Press, 1989.**

This handsome book is "a highly personal narrative about a group of paintings through the eyes, hands, and minds of the artists themselves."

Swentzell, Rina. *Children of Clay: A Family of Pueblo Potters.* **We Are Still Here Series: Native Americans Today. Minneapolis: Lerner Publications, 1992.**

Another award-winning book embracing Native artistic traditions of earth and clay in harmony with life.

Thomas, David Hurst. *Native American Archaeology: A Guide to Exploring Ancient North American Cultures.* **New York: Prentice Hall, 1994.**

Through an examination of ruins, artifacts, and more, this book describes ancient Native American cultures from a number of tribes in the United States and Canada. Illustrated.

Waldman, Carl. *Atlas of the North American Indian.* **New York: Facts on File, 1985.**

Organized by topic, this volume studies Native American history and culture.

————. *Encyclopedia of Native American Tribes.* **New York: Facts on File, 1988.**

A fascinating reference work covering more than 150 native tribes in North America; beautifully illustrated.

Weatherford, Jack. *Indian Givers: How the Indians of the Americas Transformed the World.* **New York: Crown, 1988.**

Details Native American contributions to modern society.

Welch, James. *Riding the Earthboy*. **New York: World Publishing Co., 1971.**

This moving collection of forty-six poems, "rich in the imagery of the land and Indian life," established James Welch early in the forefront of American poets and writers.

Whitehorse, David. *Pow-Wow: The Contemporary Pan-Indian Celebration*. **San Diego: San Diego State University, 1988.**

A beautifully written and illustrated book by the author, who is Sicangu Sioux, Southern Comanche, and Irish. He is from the Lower Brule River Reservation in South Dakota, and is a teacher and powwow dancer.

Wittstock, Laura Waterman. *Ininatig's Gift of Sugar: Traditional Native Sugarmaking*. **We Are Still Here Series: Native Americans Today. Minneapolis: Lerner Publications, 1993.**

The colorful task of sugaring in late winter, and the rich traditions surrounding this ancient harvest, are explored with wonderful photographs by Dale Kakkak.

Chapter 2
Why Trace Your Roots?

"Mitaku Oyasin—With all beings and all things we shall be as relatives."
—Black Elk, Oglala Sioux holy man

"Be strong of mind, O chiefs: Carry no anger and hold no grudges. Think not forever of yourselves, O chiefs, nor of your own generation. Think of continuing generations of our families, think of our grandchildren and those yet unborn, whose faces are coming from beneath the ground."
—Deganawidah, the Iroquois peacemaker

You are the unique result of many ingredients that determined some things about you before you were born. The color of your hair and eyes, the pigment of your skin, your height and body type come, in part, from your genetic codes: your genes. Other characteristics, like the accent of your speech, your views about life and the world, and the school you attend, are a result of ever-changing influences. Environmental factors certainly affect who you are and how your life develops within and beyond your family. The various foods you eat can affect your moods and emotional responses by their subtle chemical changes within your body.

Do you fly off the handle easily? You may find that some of your kinfolk were also a bit high-strung, or that flashes of quick anger are your family's way of dealing with frustration. Perhaps there is a family history of digestive problems that cause irritability. Many Native Americans have lactose intolerance, which is an inability to digest milk and most dairy products.

While Native Americans today live in both rural and urban areas, traditional Native American peoples lived and worked in conjunction with natural seasons and cycles. If you consider yourself a nature-lover, this may be a personal connection to your Native American heritage. Above, Native American warriors keep watch in the stunningly beautiful setting of what is today Glacier National Park in Montana.

Special talents are also passed along through the generations. Do you have a sharp mind for numbers? Do you have musical talent? Do you like to dance? Are you a fine athlete? Are you a great cook? Perhaps you have a great sense of humor, are a fine storyteller, or are the class clown. Perhaps learning of a great-grandfather's involvement with traditional medicine will fuel your own ambition to attend medical school. When you trace your roots, you embark on a fascinating adventure. Genealogical research is a detailed way to learn more about yourself. Sometimes, looking back over your ancestry and origins can help you more successfully move into your future. As you look at your family's many traits, appreciate the beneficial ones that have been passed along to you, and work carefully with the ones that concern you so that they are less influential in your life.

Along with these valuable reasons, people also want to trace their Native American roots because of the personal satisfaction of establishing one's identity as part of a larger family within a community or nation. We are living in a period of increasing national and ethnic pride. Many of our ancestors have lived through generations of suppressed pride and persecution, yet have fiercely maintained a sense of who they are. Many others have found it difficult to hold onto Native American traditions. You may find that some of your kinfolk are not interested in exploring details of the family's genealogy. It is best to proceed carefully and be sensitive to family members' feelings.

You may research your roots in order to establish your background for enrollment in a Native American tribe, or to gain affiliation with the tribe's culture and work. Many of us find that we have mixed ethnic heritage and can chart our Native American ancestry in a number of ways, yet not specifically enough to quality for tribal enrollment. However, the knowledge gained and the resources and sensitivities gathered from genealogical research are important enough by themselves.

You may research your Native American roots in order to fill in the empty spaces in your family tree, and to better understand your ancestors' migrations and lifeways. Tracing your kinfolks' movements, or lack of them, can be fascinating work. Whatever your reasons for tracing your roots, you have embarked on an exciting personal quest that can last a lifetime.

Learning About Your Origins

Learning about where you come from is another way of understanding history and geography. You may need to be a "super sleuth" to do some of this tracking. Some of the limbs and branches of your family tree may open out clearly, allowing you to trace family lines back for generations, even centuries. Other branches may be blank and seem almost to resist investigation. Several of my family lines are like that. In one case I learned that my Hornaday relatives created their own surname. Where did they come from? What were they trying to hide, or hide from? I still cannot answer some of the simple questions like these. With luck, you will not run into such problems, yet if you do, perhaps it will make your research more interesting and challenging.

Those people from whom we are descended, our forebears, our ancestors, are the ones we are looking for as we trace our roots. You are a "twig" on your family tree. Begin with what you know and progress backward through time on your quest for your ancestors. If we could ever accurately trace our family tree back to the beginning of time, we might see that we are all interrelated.

Getting Started

Developing your own personal history—your genealogy— begins with you and fans out to include your parents and their parents. The basics of genealogy are: *who* (use full name, including each woman's maiden name or family name), *when* (dates of births, marriages, and deaths), and *where* (the place where each key event occurred). You can lay this out in several ways as you compile your family's information. Forms and charts, such as pedigree charts and family group sheets, have been developed to help you organize genealogical records. You can make your own versions of these charts to accommodate your kinfolk and show your descent information. An example of a pedigree chart, and instructions on how to complete it, appear later in this book.

The descending generations of your own unique kinship follow a pattern of surnames. A surname, or last name, is the name that you share with other family members, as distinguished from your first name. In recording this pattern, the father's name is written above the mother's name, with their birth dates and birthplaces written just beneath their names and their marriage dates and places written between them, or under the father's dates, followed by dates and places of death. As you gather your family history and write it out in a vertical and horizontal chart, you will have your paternal (father's) descent line across the upper half of the page and your maternal (mother's) descent line across the lower half of the page. Begin with this immediate, vital information. It is intriguing to put information about yourself and your family on paper, opening the channels of your own personal history.

Next, interview your parents and grandparents, if you can, about this project and the information you need. Communicating with your family members is vital to the success of your family history project, and you may find kinfolk you did not even know about before you started. You may be lucky enough to find another genealogist in the family. Most enjoy sharing their research work and even brainstorming with you on how to track down hard-to-find details. You may unearth some real treasures and open valuable channels of correspondence with family members you have never met.

You may enjoy "chatting" on the Internet about your family research project, and for many special details you will want to delve into some of the valuable books and records (listed in the **Resources** sections following each chapter of this book) that can help to deepen your search and broaden your understanding. Above all, enjoy these various processes. Tracing family roots brings history into clearer focus. As you discover more about where you came from and learn about some of the kinfolk from your past, you will develop a rich feeling for your American heritage and your own place in history.

There will come a time when you have gathered all that you can and processed it as well as possible. At that point you will need to explore other avenues of help. You may want to verify some of the family information you have already gathered. It is not unusual to hear conflicting stories about some kinfolk. We can sometimes learn much through family folklore, but how do we know if it is true? We need to turn to other resources, such as those listed later in this book, for documentation and help.

Staying Organized

It is valuable to this process of gathering information to keep good records from the very beginning and to use fairly standard forms. You can make your own forms on lined notebook paper to begin with. You may be able to find examples of the various forms at your library or school. You can even buy forms, charts, and workbooks from various genealogical societies and publishers. These genealogical forms are discussed further in chapter 8.

As you become more interested in the family information that you find, you'll be pleased to have the forms and files in which to record it. Set up a good simple system: a notebook, a file, or both. When a family member gives you an old photograph or some valuable information, write down the date, who gave it to you, and what was said about it. Later, another family member might look at the same old photo and identify some of the individuals differently, or remember who was missing, or recall something more about the time and circumstances surrounding the picture. Add this to the same file with corresponding notes and dates of information received. Even contradictions can be fascinating.

Resources

GENERAL REFERENCE SOURCES

Brandon, William. *The American Heritage Book of Indians.* **New York: Dell, 1984.**

This comprehensive source has particularly good coverage of the history of relations between Indians and whites.

Curtis, Natalie, ed. *The Indian Book.* **New York: Harper Publishers, 1935.**

A classic compendium of folklore, songs, poetry, historical sketches, and much more.

Davis, Mary B., ed. *Native America in the Twentieth Century: An Encyclopedia.* **New York: Garland Publishing, 1994.**

An excellent resource on numerous tribes and cultural fine points.

Grumet, Robert S., ed. *Working Together to Preserve the Past.* **Cultural Resource Management (CRM), Vol. 18(7). Washington, DC: U.S. Department of the Interior National Park Service Cultural Resources, 1995.**

Select papers on historic contacts in the Northeast, with fascinating cultural and archaeological updates by noted authorities.

Hammond World Atlas. **Vol. 1. Maplewood, NJ: Hammond, 1991.**

Definitive historic maps detailing important phases in Native American settlements under history's relentless pressures and changes. Excellent documentation of resettlement changes and movements.

Hodge, Frederick W., ed. *Handbook of American Indians North of Mexico.* **New York: Pageant Books, 1960.**

Valuable encyclopedia, with descriptive information on many tribes.

Klein, Barry T. *Reference Encyclopedia of the American Indian.* **6th ed. West Nyack, NY: Toll Publishers, 1993.**

More than 670 pages of tribal councils, reservations, tribal groups, and national associations, including Alaska and Canada, plus valuable bibliographies and biographies.

McNickle, D'Arcy. *Indian Tribes of the United States: Ethnic and Cultural Survival.* **New York: Oxford University Press, 1962.**

A view of Native American and Anglo-American cultural differences and failures in adjustment and understanding.

Potter, Dorothy W. *Southeastern Pioneers, Passports of 1770–1823: Indian, Spanish, and Other Land Passports for Tennessee, Kentucky, Georgia, Mississippi, Virginia, North and South Carolina.* **Baltimore: Genealogical Publishing Co., 1994.**

Fascinating, detailed reference guide for this unique period of history in the South.

Waldman, Carl. *Encyclopedia of Native American Tribes.* **New York: Facts on File, 1988.**

Discusses more than 150 Indian tribes of North America.

Wood, Marion. *Ancient America: Cultural Atlas for Young People.* **New York: Facts on File, Equinox Books, 1990.**

Excellent illustrations supplement this detailed cultural history of the Americas, with valuable time lines spanning more than 3,000 years.

Woodhead, Henry, ed. *The American Indians Series.*
Alexandria, VA: Time-Life Books, 1993.

> Richly illustrated, well-researched accounts, with
> thoughtful perspectives and details.

GETTING STARTED

Allen, Desmond Walls, and Billingsley, Carolyn Earle.
Beginner's Guide to Family History Research. **Bounti-**
ful, UT: American Genealogical Lending Library, 1991.

> A fine introduction to family history research. Includes
> numerous examples and specific chapters on organization,
> researching in archives and libraries, use of census
> records, and conducting interviews and genealogical cor-
> respondence.

American Genealogy: A Basic Course
National Genealogical Society
4527 17th Street North
Arlington, VA 22207-2363

> Write to the National Genealogical Society for a brochure
> about this program. It incorporates both written and video
> guides to introduce beginners to genealogical research.

Dollarhide, William. *Managing a Genealogical*
Project: A Complete Manual for the Management and
Organization of Genealogical Materials. **Baltimore:**
Genealogical Publishing Co., 1988.

> A thorough guide to organizing the vast amount of infor-
> mation you will have to store. This book is written by the
> designer of some of the most popular computer software
> for genealogical organization.

Jordan, Lewis. *Cite Your Sources: A Manual for Docu-*
menting Family Histories and Genealogical Records.
Jackson: University Press of Mississippi, 1980.

Proper citation of sources ensures accuracy in your genealogical project. This book gives advice on how to make clear citations for a variety of genealogical sources.

Parker, Kenneth B. *Find Your Roots: A Beginner's Kit for Tracing Your Family Tree*. Southfield, MI: Lezell-Brasch Associates, 1977.

A useful tool for beginning genealogists. Includes sample ancestry charts and family group sheets for you to photocopy or use as a model when creating your own.

Chapter 3
Celebrating Heritage and Diversity

"The cultural 'package' that each of us is born into differs from other cultural 'packages.' I emerged from between two cultural 'packages'—American and Native American. I was born of mixed-blood parents and did not grow up within the social structure of a native community. However, my mother did plant within me some strong seeds of traditional sensitivities."

—Helen A. Attaquin, Gay Head Wampanoag historian and elder from Martha's Vineyard, Massachusetts, 1985

Tracing the ancestry of your family can be an emotional, exciting process as you celebrate your family's history, looking with sensitivity at your kinfolk over the decades. Do not be judgmental. Whatever you may find, maintain the outlook that your kinfolk were doing the best they could under the circumstances of their lives and times. Browse through some of the biographies and autobiographies that follow chapter 8 to gain an appreciation for the ways in which other Native Americans have faced and overcome life's challenges.

Researching your family history will give you a new sense of belonging. As you learn more about where you came from, and how you got here, you create a secure place in history. Perhaps your project will tie up a lot of loose threads and help to knit some family members more closely together.

Family history is a compelling study that brings our many kinfolk together in a pedigree, a register recording the clearly laid out lines of your ancestors and descendants. Genealogical societies and many Native American tribes require a documentation of pedigree for tribal enrollment.

Genealogical research will require you to study your own family unit as well as those of your ancestors. Consider how family groupings have changed over the generations. Above, a family sits outside of their traditional mud-and-stick home on a New Mexico reservation in 1967.

Kinship is the basis of families, and members belong by birth, by marriage, and by formal and informal adoption. Family units sometimes embrace close friends who become included as kin even though no formal attachments or legalities exist. Perhaps there is such a person in your family—a special godparent, "uncle," "aunt," or "cousin" who means a great deal to you, yet is not a blood relative.

Where Did It All Begin?

At the dawn of civilization, families joined together in small units to form bands, clans, and phratries (large kinship groups), which eventually became tribes. Some tribes coalesced into confederacies and leagues, banding together for peaceful protection and as trading partners. Some tribes became patriarchies, centered around their male leaders, and others were matriarchies, centered around the elder women, who often chose the male leaders. In Native American societies, women were often leaders. This tradition continues today as many Native American women distinguish themselves in leadership roles, along with Native American men who are chiefs and leaders, captains of industry, college and museum presidents, and members of congress.

Nontraditional Families

Many of us have lived in families with only one parent, or in the household of another relative or a grandparent. Regardless of your family circumstances, it is normal to be curious about your past and family background. You may know the name and background of only one of your birth parents, yet conducting family history research for this one area of your ancestry can be very valuable. Choosing your challenges carefully and sensitively, you may be able to get a great deal of information from the parent or family member you live with. As your research work blossoms, you might connect with other relatives and family members. You may be able to learn more about your absent parent, but if that is not possible, your family research work can still continue.

I can still remember the joy of finding and reconnecting

with my dear paternal cousins, aunts, uncles, and other kinfolk a few years ago. I felt that I had "lost them" for sure—more than forty years ago, back in my childhood, when my mother and father were divorced. It never occurred to me that they might have wondered about me, too, and the rest of our family. It is so exciting to catch up on lost time. Visiting by telephone and letters, we covered the missing forty years and worked collectively to trace our family roots. My birth father had lost touch with the family, but a search of the social security records and a death certificate proved that he had died some years back.

Adoption

A number of my friends are adopted and do not know who their birth parents are. What do you do in such a case? Within our legal system, adoption of an infant or child by a person or family gives that child the privileges, rights, and responsibilities of one's biological offspring. Along with privileges, however, come often-unforeseen problems. Many Native American tribes are opposed to allowing their infants and children to be adopted by outsiders and brought up outside of their cultural heritage. Legal issues and entanglements have flared up in several tribal areas, and these are very sensitive issues.

Native American families sometimes act as foster parents, taking in children and babies from their tribe and caring for them. Dale and Mary Rose Weasel in Little Eagle, South Dakota, on the Standing Rock Sioux Reservation, have long been foster parents. Along with bringing up their own children, they have welcomed other Native children in their community into their family embrace. Like other traditional families, they work to teach and share with their nonbiological children the native arts, crafts, music, and philosophies that they enjoy. Still other children are adopted by new families and brought up far from their origins, facing new opportunities and challenges, and learning to "walk in two worlds."

If you are adopted, you have twice the opportunity to

conduct research on your background. You are now a part of your adoptive family's history, and by learning more of this you may gain a stronger sense of belonging within this family. You may also be able to trace your biological family's roots, although this might prove to be quite a challenge. It is normal to be curious about your birth parents. Legally, birth-parent records are sealed at least until the adoptee is eighteen years of age. This was meant to be a mutually protective law, sensitive to all parties' needs. It is best to talk to your adoptive parents first to see if they will help you begin this search. If you know your tribe, or a relative's name, or if you know the state or region in which you were born, you can use some of the guidelines in this book to begin your research.

Adoptees make up 2 percent of the American population, and this proportion may continue to grow. Adoptees, once they are eighteen, have legal access to biological family records in most states. They can even sign up on adoption registers to be matched with their birth parents, if their birth parents have also registered. A number of books and societies can assist with your quest if you are patient and persistent. John Homer, director of the Western American Indian Chamber in Denver, was adopted by non-Indian parents as a child. He later decided to research and document his lineage. After successfully proving his ancestry, he gained membership in the Chickasaw Tribe.

Resources

ADOPTEE SUPPORT ORGANIZATIONS

Adopted and Searching/Adoptee-Birthparent Reunion
  Registry
401 East 74th Street
New York, NY 10021
212-988-0110

Adoptees and Birthparents in Search
P.O. Box 5551
West Columbia, SC 29171
803-796-4508

Adoptee's Liberty Movement Association (ALMA)
850 Seventh Avenue
New York, NY 10019
212-581-1568

> This is the foremost group in activism for adoptees' rights
> to information, and they have one of the first reunion
> registries.

Adoptees Together
Route 1, Box 30-B-5
Climax, NC 27233

Adoptive Families of America
3333 Highway 100 North
Minneapolis, MN 55422
800-372-3300 (24-hour hotline)

American Adoption Congress
1000 Connecticut Avenue NW
Washington, DC 20036

American Indian Adoption Resource Exchange
Council of Three Rivers American Indian Center
200 Charles Street
Pittsburgh, PA 15238
412-782-4457

National Adoption Information Clearinghouse
11426 Rockville Pike
Rockville, MD 20852

INFORMATION ON ADOPTION

Cohen, Shari. *Coping with Being Adopted*. New York: Rosen Publishing Group, 1988.

A general guide for teenagers who feel stress in their family and social lives because they do not know or live with their biological parents. Includes a chapter on the pros and cons of searching for your birth parents.

Dorris, Michael. *The Broken Cord: A Family's Ongoing Struggle with Fetal Alcohol Syndrome*. New York: Harper & Row, 1989.

A Native American scholar tells the deeply moving story of his adopted son, Adam, who suffered from fetal alcohol syndrome. He needed to find out about his adopted son's birth parents to unravel the puzzle of his son's medical condition.

Falke, Joseph. *Everything You Need to Know about Being a Foster Child*. New York: Rosen Publishing Group, 1995.

The breakup of the family as a result of drugs, violence, poverty, and neglect has reached epidemic proportions. Tactics for dealing with a sense of dislocation as well as techniques for settling in as a foster child are provided.

Gouke, Mary Noel. *One-Parent Children: The Growing Minority*. New York: Garland, 1990.

A resource guide for the common situation of being the child of a single parent. Includes interviews with children, teenagers, parents, and counselors for input on how to cope.

Kingsolver, Barbara. *Pigs in Heaven*. New York: HarperCollins, 1989.

A deeply felt novel of love between a mother and her adopted Cherokee daughter, Turtle, and the complex web connecting their future, their past, and the Cherokee Nation in Oklahoma.

Krementz, Jill. *How It Feels to Be Adopted*. New York: Knopf, 1982.

Family and genealogy are sensitive issues that can raise many questions. This book explains the special problems encountered by adoptees through interviews with child and adult adoptees. The author describes her own experience, including curiosity about birth parents, school-age social stigmas, and a confused sense of self.

Nash, Renea D. *Coping as a Biracial/Biethnic Teen*. New York: Rosen Publishing Group, 1995.

Teens of mixed ethnicity may face special issues as they decide which parts of their background to focus on in a genealogical search. This book details biracial backgrounds and shows how to celebrate diversity while developing an ethnic identity. Focuses on the best of both worlds, while examining some of the dilemmas involved.

Pearson, Carol Lynn. *One on the Seesaw: The Ups and Downs of a Single-Parent Family*. New York: Random House, 1988.

Offers guidance, celebrates the positive aspects of this special relationship, and discusses the difficulties involved, including dealing with a missing parent.

People Searching News

Periodical for adoptees and birth parents, published by J. E. Carlson & Associates, P.O. Box 22611, Ft. Lauderdale, FL 33335; 305-370-7100. Includes updates on adoptions, advocacy groups, birth parent/adoptee registries, and articles by adoptees about their experiences seeking their heritage and birth families.

Sadler, Judith DeBoard. *Families in Transition: An Annotated Bibliography*. **Hamden, CT: Archon Books, 1988.**

> Guide to resources in the United States for all kinds of alternative families, including single parents, unmarried couples, foster care, and stepfamilies. May prove a helpful reference for genealogical research.

Social Security Administration
Office of Central Records Operations
Baltimore, MD 21201

> Request form SSA-L997 to find a living relative by ordering his or her social security application. Not all requests will be honored; because this material is classified, the administration has the right to decide whether the request is warranted.

Social Security Administration Death Master File

This record of recently deceased Americans is available in microfilm from the Family History Centers of the Church of Jesus Christ of Latter-day Saints. Check with your nearest branch.

Wagonseller, Bill R.; Ruegamer, Lynne C.; and Harrington, Marie C. *Coping in a Single-Parent Home*. **New York: Rosen Publishing Group, 1995.**

> Learn to view your single-parent upbringing as a whole alternative family, rather than a traditional family missing

a piece. This book offers advice on dealing with divorce and separation of the parents, and the teen's feelings of abandonment and guilt associated with an absent parent. This situation may have implications for family history research.

Witherspoon, Mary Ruth. "How to Conduct an Adoption Search." *Everton's Genealogical Search*, **July/ August 1994, p. 10.**

An up-to-date essay on the difficulties and rewards of trying to find your biological family lines, written by a person who found some 300 living relatives. Although the author documents the discouragements she encountered, her final message is: "It's worth it, so don't give up!"

Chapter 4
A Deeper Sense of History

"We have lived upon this land from days beyond history's records, far past any living memory, deep into the time of legend. The story of my people and the story of this place are one single story. No man can think of us without thinking of this place. We are always joined together."
—A Taos Pueblo man, 1968, in an appeal for the return of Blue Lake

The land of your ancestors is alive with ancient monuments, impressive ruins, and the ancient prehistoric presence of many earlier cultures. The Americas have been peopled with succeeding waves of hunters and gatherers for perhaps 40,000 years, although there is scant evidence from more than 12,000 years ago. From the Arctic Ocean, following the Cordillero Blanca Mountains—the spine of the Americas—to the tip of South America, more than 9,000 miles measures and binds these two dynamic continents together. This giant backbone of volcanic vertebrae includes the Rocky Mountains and the Andes, diverse homelands to strikingly different native peoples.

Mesoamerica, the middle regions of Mexico and Central America, embraced the flowering of the Olmec, Toltec, and Maya peoples, who constructed immense, sophisticated city-states around hundreds of stone temples and pyramids. These city-states were centers for many thousands of early peoples. The later Aztec inherited much of their horticultural wisdom and continued to build their own farming and trading empires. Elaborate networks linked many of these urban centers, as they reached out to include nature in harmony with the cosmos. Their view of the universe placed earth between thirteen heavens and nine levels of the underworld.

A colossal Olmec basalt sculpture of a helmeted head, unearthed at San Lorenzo in southern Mexico, weighs more than twenty tons and stands more than nine feet high. It may date from 1200 BC and be associated with one of Mesoamerica's earliest known political and religious centers. Is this the face of one of your earliest ancestors? An amazing array of Mayan rulers, priests, priestesses, and their captives are chiseled in semiprecious stone, carved into native stone stelae, and painted on ancient clay ceremonial pots. Are some of these your ancestors?

A life-size stone carving of Xochipilli—the Aztec Prince of Flowers, patron of poetry, love, music, and dance—wears an ornate, crested mask and headdress as he sits cross-legged on his beautifully carved stone throne. Perhaps one of your ancestors worked to create this prehistoric masterpiece. He seems to echo the Aztec poetic lament translated from the "Songs of Huexotzingo":

> "Will I leave only this: Like the flowers that wither? Will nothing last in my name—Nothing of my fame here on earth? At least flowers! At least song!"

Ancient Inca farmers terraced steplike fields, supported by stone walls, cut by carefully laid stone steps and drainage channels. These early gardeners were the first to cultivate potatoes, peanuts, cotton, and various grain crops, along with making some of the finest textiles in the world. The Inca Empire radiated out from their great capital Cuzco, where the Temple of the Sun guarded the ceremonial heart of their government. Less than fifty miles northwest stands Machu Picchu, the ruins of one of the world's most spectacular ancient sites, where mountain farmers constructed nearly 300 buildings of closely fitted stone, grouped along the sides of an oblong plaza.

The Nazca people from the southern coast of Peru and the Moche people from the northern coast of Peru have left us dazzling reminders of their ancient cultures, which continue to puzzle scholars who study their prehistoric sites. Temples and pyramids of the Moche reflect a sophisticated ceremonial concept, and their Huaca del Sol, Temple of the Sun, is probably the largest adobe building in the Americas. The Nazca Lines are among the most fascinating archaeological puzzles, covering almost 200 square miles of desert in patterns that seem to reveal complex solar alignments.

Ancient North America

Ceremonial centers, burial mounds, and remarkable earthworks stretch across the broad middle heartland of North America. Those who built them are known as the Mound Builders. The Mississippian Mound City of Cahokia includes more than 100 mounds grouped around plazas; it was the largest prehistoric city north of Mexico until about 1100 AD. (Remnants of the civilization are still visible, located near East St. Louis in Illinois.) The earlier Adena and Hopewell cultures constructed hundreds of mounds spreading across eastern North America and left us masterpieces of artistry. These early farming cultures also created the famous 1,300-foot long Serpent Mound winding along a hilltop in what is now southern Ohio. Was this a sacred image, and perhaps a creation figure?

By about 1000 BC, the ancient Americans we now call the Mound Builders were increasingly successful hunters and gatherers and had begun to farm a number of food crops: sunflowers and other grains, along with various squashes and gourds. By about 100 BC the Hopewell people were growing maize, the prolific "gold of the Americas" that we now call corn, throughout the fertile Mississippi Valley. Corn was first cultivated by the Mesoamericans almost 7,000 years ago and spread along early trade routes for millennia throughout Middle America. Scientists recognize this region as one of the world's great centers of agriculture.

These early ancestors of today's Native Americans left haunting reminders of their technical artistry and the importance of the sacred in their lives. As we read the prolific archaeological evidence from their sophisticated civilizations, we must realize that we are finding only scant remnants of what they once were.

The Red Paint People, who lived along what is now coastal northern New England and eastern Canada almost 3,000 years ago, are noted for their extensive use of ground red iron ore to cover their tools and burials. Anthropologists maintain that the people had very sacred beliefs about the uses of this native ore. Red continues to be a sacred color to most Native American peoples today.

Native American Culture Areas

Culture areas are specific geographical regions where various Native American groups and tribes had (and have) similar lifeways and shared some things in common, such as related languages and artistic similarities. Environment and geography are major factors in determining the diverse native culture areas in North America, and each region has long been populated by native peoples, who are often quite different from one another. Many native groups have their own unique "stories of origin"—explaining where and how they have come to be where they are now. History and prehistory show us that native peoples have been continually evolving on this continent for longer than we may realize, and judging from the archaeological evidence to date, we think that we know quite a bit about their cultures. The concept of culture embraces many aspects of life, from survival and subsistence patterns to art, language, spiritual beliefs, social and political organizations, and technology. Based on certain shared cultural characteristics, we divide North America into distinct Native American Culture Areas.

Starting at the top of the map of North America, within the Arctic Circle, and moving southward and then from west to east, and back to the southwest in a zigzag, we have the Arctic, Subarctic, Northwest Coast, Plateau, Great Plains, Northeast, Southeast, Great Basin, Southwest, California, Mesoamerica, and Latin America (Caribbean) Culture Areas. These twelve areas are each populated by many Native American groups, bands, and tribes, and throughout the

An Inuit man drills ivory with a drill suspended from his chin. The Inuit live throughout the Arctic region, including Alaska, Canada, and Siberia.

course of time, populations have shifted and changed almost constantly. (Some of these areas have distinctly drawn boundaries, whereas others are more variable; you may find different configurations in other reference books.)

The Arctic Culture Area stretches from coastal Greenland Island in the extreme northeast, spanning more than 5,000 miles of rugged northern regions, from northern Canada and Alaska, to the Aleutian Islands and Siberia. This extreme northern environment, beyond the treeline, touches five oceans: the Atlantic, Arctic, Beaufort Sea, Bering Sea, and Pacific, and has been inhabited for perhaps 5,000 years by native peoples who call themselves the Yup'ik, Inuit, Iglulik, Netsilik, Sallirmuit, and Aleut. Today they also bear the names of the regions where they live, such as Polar Eskimo, Labrador Coast Inuit, Bering Strait Inuit, and so on. These diverse groups developed remarkable lifeways within this starkly beautiful environment of windswept tundras frequently covered with ice and snow, reaching from the polar extremes to the vast Hudson Bay regions. Interaction between Arctic, Subarctic, and Northwest Coast Cultures was shaped by frequent and seasonal trading needs. Encounters with European settlers brought both disease and economic turmoil for many of the native groups, and these ramifications continue to affect native peoples.

The Subarctic Culture Area stretches across the whole of North America from Newfoundland's Atlantic shores in the northeast to north-central Alaska and Cook's Inlet on the Pacific coast, and encompasses perhaps 2 million square miles of rugged geographical terrain and environmental diversity. Windswept tundras and dense coniferous woods are spotted with swamps, bogs, and ponds and cut by numerous streams and rivers feeding into huge lakes. These diverse ecosystems are the homelands of the Cree, Montagnais, Naskapi, and other Algonquian language speakers, along with (moving west) the Northern Ojibway, Beaver, Slavey, Dogrib, Yellowknife, Tanana, Koyukon, and many more.

Throughout the settlement periods of these last four centuries, economic, political, and resource needs and pressures have changed native lifeways both for good and bad. The James Bay Cree in eastern Canada have garnered considerable public support for their "Save James Bay" campaign against a Canadian hydroelectric project that would flood and destroy their broad homelands.

The Northwest Coast Culture Area hugs more than 2,000 rugged miles of Pacific Coastal and Cascade Mountain regions from the Alaskan Panhandle to northern California. Lush temperate environments with abundant rainfall and diverse wild resources once sustained dense settlements of dynamic tribes. This is the land and the people of totem poles, potlatches (ceremonial feasts), and immense war canoes—emblems of successful whaling and fishing tribes—who often lavished their accumulated wealth upon their relatives, neighboring tribes, and even their enemies. Tlingit, Tsimshian, Haida, Gitksan, Bella Bella, Bella Coola, Kwakiutl, and Nootka peoples populated the northern reaches and created great plank houses and powerful artwork that is some of the most spectacular in North America. Farther south, in Washington and Oregon coastal regions, the Makah, Quileute, Quinault, Clallam, Chehalis, Salish, Chinook, and Siletz tribes and many others hunted, fished, and gathered nature's bounty as their villages grew and prospered. Early contacts with Russian fur traders in the 1700s and 1800s brought challenges to survival for most of these villages, many of which succumbed to deadly diseases to which the native people had no immunity. Christian missionaries and government pressures further altered some of their most vital lifeways, like their generous potlatch traditions, which were outlawed. European settlers exploited salmon and halibut reserves and disrupted native means of survival like whaling, timbering, sealing, and hunting, thereby seriously undermining the native economies and survival mechanisms.

The California Culture Area encompasses most of the state of California, extending down the Baja peninsula of Mexico along more than 1,200 miles of stunning coastline.

Wildly contrasting environments here stretch from the Death Valley Desert, the lowest point in North America, to the highest point in the forty-eight contiguous states, Mount Whitney in the Sierras. Lush botanical resources of six environmental zones served to support more than fifty Indian tribes, perhaps the most dense native settlements in North America north of Mesoamerica. These regions are homelands of the Tolowa, Yurok, Shasta, Karok, Hupa, Maidu, Pomo, and Miwok, as well as other tribes. Central and southern regions are homelands of the Esselen, Mono, Yokut, Chumash, Serrano, Luiseno, Cahuilla, Diegueno, and other tribes. Variable climates and bountiful resources drew many hunters and gatherers to these regions more than 20,000 years ago. Amid the wealth of wild edible foods, the carbohydrate-rich acorns were a staple of native life and were processed into soups, gruels, and breads. Abundant resources enabled native populations to increase and thrive, and these tribes developed complex baskets, tools, and ceremonial accoutrements representing their rich spiritual beliefs. These aspects were little understood by the early Spanish adventurers and missionaries who encountered these tribes during the colonial period. Centuries of conflict and exploitation of the region's resources have greatly diminished and displaced California tribal populations.

The Plateau Culture Area straddles the Continental Divide and covers about 200,000 square miles from central British Columbia south through eastern Washington and Oregon, and across northern Idaho to northwestern Montana. Verdant valleys laced by turbulent rivers rich with migrating salmon, trout, whitefish, and sturgeon supported the Lillooet, Shuswap, Okanagan, Kootenai, Colville, Kalispel, Columbia, and Klickitat tribes. The southern regions were the homelands of the Yakima, Klamath, Modoc, Walla Walla, Cayuse, Nez Perce, Coeur D'Alene, Spokane, and Flathead tribes, who hunted, fished, and traded across this expansive area and beyond. These regions were probably settled by the ancestors of today's tribes more than 8,000 years ago, and they steadily evolved successful subsistence economies.

The Great Basin Culture Area is a huge natural desert stretching some 250,000 square miles from the Sierra Nevada mountain range in eastern California to the Rocky Mountains. These high arid environments include southern Oregon and Idaho, and all of Nevada and Utah. This area was sparsely populated by the Paiute, Shoshone, Ute, Bannock, Gosiute, Washo, Mono, Panamint, and Chemehuevi tribes and subgroups. Sagebrush, juniper, and pinion pine dominate these landscapes, growing above important plants such as bitterroot, camas, wild onion, and Indian potato. Many of the Great Basin tribes were called "Digger Indians" by early contacts, who observed their seasonal dependence on various wild resources.

The Southwest Culture Area (often called the Desert Southwest) reaches from southern Utah and Colorado southward across Arizona, New Mexico, and western portions of Texas well into Mexico—boasting some of the most striking topography in North America. From the deeply cut Grand, Zion, and Bryce Canyons, to the jutting mesas of the Colorado Plateau, south to the torrid Sonoran Desert, and straddling mountains and ancient cliff dwellings—this broad region is resonant with antiquity. Ancestors of today's tribes first settled these homelands more than 12,000 years ago. Hopi, Navajo, Zuni, Apache, Havasupai, Hualapai, Mojave, Maricopa, Cocopa, Papago, and Pima peoples share these environments with nineteen distinctive Pueblo Peoples in New Mexico. The Pima Bajo, Seri, Yaqui, Mayo, and Tarahumara, along with many other tribes, stretch southward, deeper into central Mexico. As with the tribes of other culture areas, these tribes share many similarities, yet are strikingly different from one another. From snow-capped mountaintops to fertile river valleys, this great region supported many transitional hunting and gathering economies and welcomed the earliest horticulture of corn, squash, beans, cotton, tobacco, chilies, sunflowers, and much more.

The Great Plains Culture Area embraces the heartland of

North America, stretching across wind-swept grasslands and prairies and the arid southern "Badlands." It extends from the Mississippi River Valley, north and west to the Rocky Mountains, and from Saskatchewan, Manitoba, and Alberta, Canada in the north to south-central Texas. Enveloping the sacred Black Hills in South Dakota and Wyoming, as well as striking plateaus and buttes cut by numerous river systems, this region is the homeland of more than twenty tribes, many known as dynamic horse-cultures and tipi-dwellers. (When people think about Indians, they usually visualize the classic Plains Indians, who were both immortalized and misrepresented in American and European movies dealing with "cowboys and Indians." Native American actors, writers, and filmmakers have been working for several generations to overcome these unfortunate stereotypes.)

Northern Plains regions supported the Sarcee, Blood, Blackfeet, Cree, Piegan, Gros Ventre, Assiniboine, and Plains Ojibway, along with the Sioux, Hidatsa, Mandan, Arikara, and Crow. Central and southern Plains regions sustained the Cheyenne, Arapaho, Ponca, Pawnee, Omaha, Oto, Missouri, Kansa, Osage, Kiowa, Quapaw, Comanche, Wichita, Tonkawa, and others for hundreds of years. Continual movement for seasonal hunting and gathering shaped the lifeways of most of these tribes, while others settled in farming villages and raised crops of corn, squash, beans, tobacco, and sunflowers. As in other Native American culture areas, these tribes lived in distinctive dwellings and maintained extensive trading networks. Archaeological evidence shows us some aspects of this range and diversity that are quite amazing.

The Southeast Culture Area stretches east from Texas across the southlands and the Appalachian Mountains to the Atlantic, embracing most of nine southern states. Mild weather and diverse geography in the western reaches supported the Caddo, Natchez, Choctaw, Chitimacha, Tunica, Biloxi, Houma, and many neighboring tribes across Louisiana, parts of Arkansas, Oklahoma, and Mississippi. Farther southeast are the homelands of the Chickasaw, Cherokee,

Yuchi, Creek, Alabama, Seminole, Catawba, and the various tribes of the early Powhatan Confederacy. Some tribes were noted hunters, trappers, and traders, while others were farmers, weavers, and potters, fueling vast trade networks that crisscrossed many of these culture areas since early prehistoric times. Settlement by whites greatly changed these tribes' land-based economies and settlements, as many were "relocated" west of the mighty Mississippi River in Indian Territory (now eastern Oklahoma).

The Northeast Culture Area embraces the Eastern Woodlands from the Atlantic Coastal plains north into southern Canada, and west around the Great Lakes just beyond the Mississippi River. The Ojibway, Menominee, Winnebago, Sauk, Fox, Potawatomi, Kickapoo, Miami, Illinois, and Shawnee people shared the central-western regions and the land around the Great Lakes, while the Susquehanna, Delaware, Powhatan, Shinnecock, Montauk, Narragansett, Pequot, Mohegan, and Wampanoag shared southern homelands of this culture area. The Iroquois Confederacy dominated New York state and Canada, and the Wappinger and Wabenaki Confederacies dominated their northeastern regions, each composed of many unique tribes, bands, and groups of native peoples whose ancient presence stretches back more than 10,000 years.

Some authorities draw these cultural boundaries slightly differently, yet these basic culture regions help to illustrate the great diversities of native peoples and cultures in North America. As you dig deeper into native history while searching for your own roots, you will recognize how unique you are. Whether you are a member of one tribe or a descendant of several tribes, you will want to explore the **Resources** following this chapter to read about the culture, language, folklore, and environment of your ancestors.

Native American Displacement

By the time Norse and Viking explorers first reached the North American coast more than 1,000 years ago, Native American cultures had been flourishing for millennia. When

The Crow Indians, like these two schoolgirls, traditionally inhabited the Northern Plains region.

Columbus reached the Caribbean Islands in 1492, authorities estimate that between 6 and 60 million people, speaking perhaps 550 languages, inhabited North America. Some 1 to 8 million native people, speaking more than 270 different languages, lived north of what is now Mexico.

Pueblo peoples in the arid Southwest, Mound Builders in the greater Mississippi River Valley, Plains Indians across the vast prairie regions, Northwest Coast cultures along the Pacific Coast, and Algonquian and Iroquois peoples in the East had developed complex systems of government and productive yet respectful relationships with nature and its diverse resources. These widely different cultures embraced a common reverence for the land and its gifts, a proud heritage that is continually reaffirmed today through traditional ceremonies, customs, and foods.

Sadly, the Native Americans and their ways of life were not respected by the European settlers with whom they were forced to share their land. The newly formed United States Congress stated in 1789, "The utmost good faith shall always be observed towards the Indians; their land and property rights, and in liberty, they shall never be invaded or disturbed, unless in just and lawful wars authorized by Congress."

This decree proved to be an empty promise. As the East Coast became increasingly populated, the U.S. government continued to press westward, forcefully displacing Native Americans from their tribal homes. After unsuccessful attempts to negotiate the settlement of the Ohio Valley, the U.S. Army launched an attack on the Native American tribes that occupied it in 1794. This siege, the Battle of Fallen Timbers, resulted in acquiescence by the tribes to move to Indiana. But it was not long before the government decided to expand further west, and many more battles followed.

Some tribes did not go peacefully. A number of wars erupted when the government attempted to remove the Seminole from their lands in Florida. Further west, the Apache, Cheyenne, Comanche, and Sioux tribes presented militant opposition to the U.S. government's westward expansion. By 1861, the Plains Indians were forced to resort to violence in response to the advance of white settlers, when the area's buffalo herds were slaughtered. Although a combined force of Native Americans, led by a group of great war chiefs including Sitting Bull, Crazy Horse, Gall, and Two Moon, won an important victory over the army regiment of Colonel George Armstrong Custer at the Battle of Little Bighorn, they were eventually overwhelmed by the surge of white settlers. In December 1890, more than 200 members of the Miniconjou band of the Lakota were massacred at Wounded Knee—widely considered the last battle of the Indian Wars.

Although the U.S. government's primary means of assimilating Native Americans was by force, they often used more subtle measures. The Dawes General Allotment Act of 1887 divided Indian lands into private plots of 160 acres each for adult Native American individuals to farm. In exchange for complying with the act and submitting their lands for allotment, the Indian farmers would gain U.S. citizenship after they worked their plot of land for twenty-five years. This act was generally unsuccessful, as the Native Americans had no formal training in farming large plots of land and the lands they were allotted were of poor quality for farming. Many were reluctant to abandon their hunter-gatherer way of life.

The "Five Civilized Tribes"—Creek, Choctaw, Cherokee, Chickasaw, and Seminole (so called because they adapted to European ways more rapidly than other tribes)—were among the last to comply with the Dawes Act, but after the government granted portions of their land to white settlers, they had little choice in the matter. By 1900, the government succeeded in confining the remaining tribes to reservations totaling only 4 percent of all lands within the borders of the United States.

Reservation life did not treat the Native Americans well. The government offered no education to Native American children and forcefully discouraged Indian self-government.

They lent little or no aid to the Native Americans in developing economic resources on the reservation. The government was constantly reducing Native American lands, and the revenues received from these land sales never benefited the tribes themselves. As a result of these factors, Indian reservation life of the early 1900s was marked by poverty, disease, and hopelessness.

Slavery

Historical evidence exists that some Native American tribes took captives and kept slaves, usually from other tribal groups. This was especially noted among the Cherokee in the East and among various Northwest Coast peoples. There is abundant historical evidence of colonial armies killing, capturing, and enslaving hundreds of Indian captives up and down the east coast during the 1600s and 1700s. In 1713 Colonel James Moore's army, including 1,000 Indian allies, marched into Tuscarora territory in the Carolinas, killing many, and capturing 400 Tuscarora prisoners, who were sold into slavery at ten pounds sterling to help finance the campaign. This is only one of countless documented reports of this type. Various eastern tribal people, especially Narragansett, Pequot, Poosepatuck, and others, were kidnapped or captured during the colonial period and sold into slavery. Transported to the West Indies to work in sugarcane fields, or to the South to work on tobacco and cotton plantations, few were able to survive and escape, and fewer still were able to make their painful way back to their homelands.

Early Spanish, Dutch, and English encounters with various Native peoples along the eastern shores led to their capture. Pocahontas and many others suffered this fate. Stormy relations during these early centuries of contact led to the enslavement of various tribal groups. Many eastern Algonquian people were transported south to the Virgin Islands and sold into slavery to work in the sugarcane plantations.

Efforts to enslave Native Americans were rarely successful

yet always proved disastrous for native peoples. Those who did survive sometimes married African slaves, and occasionally their captors. The slavery period resulted in a mixing of bloodlines among many Indian tribes.

Migration and Extermination

Many tribes and bands disappeared because of European diseases against which they had no immunity. Early epidemics of smallpox, measles, influenza, and various respiratory infections took the lives of entire tribal villages.

The attempted extermination of the Pequot Indians by the English in 1639 in Connecticut Colony, the displacement of the Delaware Indians (the Lenni Lenape), and the migration of the Tuscarora out of the Southeast are extensively documented. The Indians suffered because of settlers' greed for their lands and resources.

Waves of migration in the late 1700s and early 1800s took many Creek, Cherokee, Chickahominy, Chickasaw, Choctaw, and Chitimacha peoples out of their homelands in the Southeast. Some refused ever to leave, and others tried to return. Most of the remaining Southeastern tribal groups were systematically finished off in the Indian Removal Act passed by the U.S. Congress in 1830. The Act targeted especially the Cherokee, Creek, Choctaw, Chickasaw, and Seminole Indians and called for the removal and relocation of eastern Indians to regions west of the Mississippi River known as Indian Territory—which is today Oklahoma. Many Oklahomans still call their state "Indian Country" or "Indian Territory" in remembrance of this period. The ramifications of this legislation sent shock waves across the land that, some say, are still being felt. The Trail of Tears during the winter of 1838–39, a forced migration ordered by President Andrew Jackson, was the systematic removal and relocation of many Cherokee, Creek, and Choctaw people to regions west of the Mississippi River. More than 17,000 Cherokee, including some of my own distant relatives, were rounded up and put in stockades and concentration camps in Georgia and Tennessee.

In 1838, tens of thousands of Cherokee, Creek, and Choctaw Indians were forced to move to regions west of the Mississippi. This event was depicted in Robert Lindneux's painting, *Trail of Tears*. Many had to make the trip on foot, and thousands did not survive the journey.

Perhaps 1,000 Cherokee escaped into the hills, and authorities estimate that another 8,000 Cherokee may have died as a result of the enforced 900-mile walk. This is just one of many such documented events in U.S. history. Today, many Native Americans will not carry a twenty-dollar bill because of the president pictured on it.

As you go more deeply into your family history, keep an open mind and realize that you are a survivor as well as a unique part of American history. Keep your balance, and remember that above all else, Native Americans have a legendary sense of humor. Most of all, Native Americans survive and thrive, and their populations are increasing.

Canada's First People

More than fifty aboriginal languages evolved in Canada, and today the 604 Canadian Indian bands strongly identify themselves according to their tribal or "First Nations" origins. In 1991, Canada estimated its indigenous population to be about 1 million out of a total population of 27.4 million.

Three distinct groups of indigenous peoples, Indian, Inuit, and Métis, are recognized in the Canadian constitution. Each group has its separate and distinct heritages, languages, cultural practices, spiritual beliefs, and contemporary concerns.

Native Canadians number about 780,000 and live throughout the country; yet the largest population concentrations are in the four western provinces and Ontario. About two-thirds of them are status, meaning that they are registered as Indians under Canada's Indian Act. "Non-status Indians are often the descendants of Indians who lost their status under various discriminatory provisions of the Indian Act (these provisions have since been repealed) or who were never registered under the Act, some by choice."*

Inuit people have occupied the northernmost regions of Canada for at least 5,000 years. In Canada, Inuit, meaning "the people," has replaced the term Eskimo. Canada may be home to about one-quarter of the world's Inuit population, estimated at 49,000 in 1991. Inuit also live in Alaska, Greenland, and Siberia.

The Métis are people of mixed Native American and European ancestry. Their numbers have grown since the eighteenth century to an estimated 200,000 in 1991, and they reside predominantly in the Prairie provinces of Manitoba, Saskatchewan, and Alberta.

Native American Tribes

The term *tribe* describes a body of people bound together by blood relationships, perhaps speaking a common language or dialect, and occupying a definite territory. A tribe may also

---

* "Canada's Aboriginal Peoples," *Canada Today/d'aujourd'hui*, Vol. 23, no. 1, 1993 (Canadian Embassy, 501 Pennsylvania Avenue NW, Washington, DC 20001), p. 3.

be socially, politically, and religiously affiliated with a village, a series of communities, or a widely scattered group of people who share a common heritage but not necessarily a tribal government. Many tribes also see themselves as nations, as they have been legally treated as tribal nations in their relationships and treaties with the U.S. government.

More than 300 federally recognized Native American tribes in the United States are located on approximately 300 federal Indian reservations. Many additional tribes and groups, almost 200, most of them east of the Mississippi River, do not have federal recognition; yet a number of them have some reservation or trust lands. Many tribes have confederated, sharing common heritages and large Western reservations.

An Indian reservation is an area of land specifically reserved for Indian use. This term comes from the early periods of the settlement of Indian lands. The establishment of reservations often followed conflicts—or attempts to avoid conflicts. During the eighteenth and nineteenth centuries most tribes were forced to relinquish their lands through various treaties that reserved a portion of land for their specific use. Countless tribal descendants still live in or near their original homelands as private family groups or communities without tribe or reservation status.

Men and women both contributed to the welfare of the tribes. The men were usually hunters, fishermen, and warriors, and the women handled food preparation and created the portable dwellings and basic family clothing. Sharing responsibilities was essential to survival and prosperity. Marriage alliances and clan and kinship ties often ensured cooperation among families, and strengthened political leadership, in some cases. In many tribes, while the men were the chosen and often hereditary leaders, family descent and ownership of certain rites and property passed through the woman's family, which is called matrilineal descent.

The matrilineal system is based upon tracing ancestral descent through the maternal line rather than through the paternal line. Some tribes were matrilocal, wherein

Anthropologists believe that the first farmers in the Southwest were women, farm plots were passed from mother to daughter, and descent was traced matrilineally. This system still survives today among the Hopi people. Above, a Hopi woman dresses the hair of an unmarried Hopi girl in the early twentieth century.

families centered their lives in the home territory of the wife's kin group or clan. Many other Native American tribes follow both the mother's and father's lines of descent in a bilateral method of determining social systems and membership.

Historically, Native American women leaders have been known as "squaw sachems" and "sunksquas," terms of great respect. The Iroquois (Haudenosaunee) tribes of upstate New York and Canada are traditional matrilineal societies. They are governed by a council of hereditary chiefs chosen by the Clan Mothers, and matrilineality determines their tribal membership and clan affiliation. Other Native American matrilineal clan systems are found among the Crow

(Absaroka) Indians of Montana, the Navajo (Dineh) of the Southwest Four Corners region, the Seminoles in Florida, Texas, and Oklahoma, and the Tlingit of the upper Northwest Coast regions of British Columbia and Alaska.

Native American patrilineal systems are found in the Kumeyaay Bands (Diegueño, Kumiai, Kamia, and Ipai/Tipai) of southern California and northwestern Mexico, Santa Clara Pueblo in the Rio Grande Valley of New Mexico, and the Quechan (Yuma) Nation in southeastern California along the Colorado River, among others.

Native American leadership concepts, while varying from tribe to tribe, largely shared the goal of building consensus within the governing group on all major matters that affected the tribe's life. Many Native American societies were governed by those who controlled a wealth of natural resources, like some of the Potlatch Peoples, the Haida, Kwakiutl, Tlingit and others among the Northwest Coast Tribes.

Native American men and women were the first leaders and diplomats on this continent, and many of their leadership concepts helped shape the foundations of the U.S. and Canadian governments. Benjamin Franklin, Thomas Jefferson, and other Founding Fathers observed Native American councils and decision-making events—principally among the Iroquois and Algonquian tribes in the Northeast. While not entirely enthusiastic about what they witnessed, they realized that strength was gained through consensus leadership.

Native American leaders representing various factions often came together in grand councils, as in the Iroquois League (Iroquois Confederacy), to strive to make peace and satisfy the majority. During the 1700s and early 1800s, many tribes in the eastern regions of Canada and the United States formed various confederacies. From the great Wabenaki Confederacy in southern Canada and northern New England, to the Wappinger Confederacy along the Hudson River Valley, to the early Powhatan Confederacy in Tidewater Virginia, hundreds of clans and tribes banded together for many reasons—especially for protection from whites and neighboring tribes. Some native confederacies were loosely woven hunting and trading networks, whereas others were quite powerful and forced tribute from other tribes outside of their regions and associations.

Fight for Rights and Independence

By the 1920s, citizens and government officials became aware of the plight of Native Americans, and significant steps were taken to improve Indian life. In 1924, the Snyder Act was passed in recognition of the Native Americans who had volunteered to serve in World War I. This act granted all Native Americans U.S. citizenship. In 1928, Congress passed the Indian Reorganization Act, consisting of sweeping reforms and the end of the allotment policy. Over the next fifty years, changes in government policy promised new rights, responsibilities, and monetary assistance for Native Americans.

Unfortunately, implementation of these new government policies was slow at best, and Native Americans grew anxious to be granted assistance and the right to govern themselves. In 1971, Indian activists formed the American Indian Movement (AIM). In the late 1960s and early 1970s, Indian unrest manifested itself in several violent episodes, including the forceful occupation of Alcatraz Island by San Francisco Indians in November 1969 and other militant takeovers and demonstrations in 1970 and 1971. In 1973, American Indian Movement members seized the Oglala Sioux village of Wounded Knee, where the U.S. Army had massacred hundreds of Indians in 1890. The protesters held out for seventy-one days, gaining much support for their cause of freedom for all American Indians. Anti-Indian racist sentiments led to several violent outbursts. The U.S. government again provided hollow promises to halt the violence and quiet angry Native American voices, but they could not be silenced forever.

In the late 1970s, the government finally began to implement policies granting rights and federal aid that had been promised to Native Americans some fifty years earlier. The

Indian Health Care Improvement Act of 1976 increased federal funding and offered professional assistance to Indian health care facilities. The Native American Relief Fund (NARF), a nonprofit Indian legal organization, won important court battles in the 1970s and 1980s, resulting in widespread changes in policy concerning over 100 Native American tribes. With the Self-Governance Demonstration Project of 1988, twenty western Indian tribes finally took the first step toward self-government by acquiring direct control of millions of dollars in federal funding. By 1992, Native Americans were exercising their self-governing powers, being freed from the last restraints of government control, and demanding equal respect and treatment.

According to the United States Bureau of the Census, the Native American population of the country is growing substantially, and many Native Americans are gravitating to the cities. The total Native American population rose from 1,420,400 in 1980 to 1,959,254 in 1990, a percentage increase of approximately 37.9. In 1995 the population was 2,226,000, and it is estimated to reach 4,346,000 in the year 2050.

Native Women Leaders

Today many Native American tribes and nations are governed by women, who, like the men, have risen to leadership roles through hard work in their communities. Serving at many different levels for both large and small tribes and native villages, these women energetically worked to promote native leadership and family needs in positive new ways. Bright, dynamic role models include Mildred I. Cleghorn, born in 1910 in captivity, leader of the Fort Sill Apaches in Oklahoma, and Betty Mae Jumper, born in 1923 at Indiantown near Lake Okeechobee in southern Florida, the first woman (beginning in 1967) to serve as chair of the Seminole Tribal Council. Wilma P. Mankiller, born in 1946 in Oklahoma of Cherokee and Dutch-Irish descent, became the first woman principal chief of the Cherokee Nation of Oklahoma in 1987. She served two four-year terms before retiring to teach; she continues to work for Indian rights. Henrietta W. Mann, born in 1934 in Clinton, Oklahoma, is a respected Cheyenne leader and educator. Beatrice A. Medicine, born in 1924 on the Standing Rock Reservation in Wakpala, South Dakota, is a scholar, educator, and author dedicated to developing Indian leadership and establishing urban Indian centers. Noted Choctaw leader and scholar Owanah Anderson, born in 1926 in Choctaw County, Oklahoma, compiled and edited *Ohoyo One Thousand: A Resource Guide of American Indian/Alaska Native Women*, which catalogs female Indian leaders, and serves as a resource guide to the women in various Indian programs.

Other notable Native American women include Menominee scholar, activist, and leader Ada Deer, born in 1935 on the Menominee Indian Reservation in northern Wisconsin. Deer, a former fellow at the Harvard Institute of Politics, John F. Kennedy School of Government, is active in state and local political organizations, and is director of the Bureau of Indian Affairs (BIA) in Washington, DC. She continues to serve as a role model and inspire individuals to become politically active. Jeanine Pease-Windy Boy-Pretty-On-Top, born in 1949 on the Colville Reservation, Washington, of Crow and German-English descent, is a leading activist, MacArthur Fellow, and the respected president of Little Big Horn College on the Crow Reservation in Montana. The former are only a few of the many Native American women whose energies have helped to create new destinies for their people. Many other Native American women are attorneys, educators, business leaders, politicians, artists, poets, and much more—often serving in several careers as well as being mothers and homemakers.

Family and Self

"Our heritage is rich and good; therein are the roots of our forebears. Use it, respect it, and be sympathetic to those who still live entirely by it."

—Ella Cara Deloria, Sioux writer and educator

Where do you place yourself and your family within the tapestry of life? Fortunately, if you proceed with thoughtfulness, yours could be a fabulous, lifelong journey.

Whatever your reasons for tracing and researching your Native American roots—and there may be many good reasons—you will want to organize the information you gather so that it makes sense (even when it doesn't seem to fit together) and so that you can refer to it easily. You might begin, as I did, with a special notebook just for family history work. I took notes while talking to relatives because I gained so much valuable information this way and enjoyed each conversation as a personal visit. Now, as I look back over those early notes, I am visiting again with those loved ones, and I can almost hear their voices. These penciled notes are filled with enthusiasm, sadness, and promise, rich details of long distances and missing years with family.

Sometimes it can be difficult to find basic information about your family unless someone recorded pertinent details in an old family Bible or album, in old quilts, or in samplers, embroidered pillows, or paintings. Quilts and other forms of stitchery often contain fragments of family history. Birth and marriage dates that were recorded nowhere else are often worked into these stitchery items. Since so many old courthouses and churches where vital records were kept have burned, especially in the South during the Civil War, we are grateful for these handmade records. Bits of poetry and key family dates are often written in favorite old books and journals, diaries, and albums. Engraved dates are occasionally found on pewter or silver trays, bowls, or cups.

I have a cousin whose uncle had written one entire branch of the family tree on a fine old white window shade, which he always took with him when he visited relatives, so that he could add more recollections and details. He even used this lovely scroll as a storytelling device.

The famous storyteller Gerard Rancourt Tsonakwa carefully chronicles his Abenaki heritage in his artwork, masks, and stories, much as his father and grandfather taught him to do. His books, tapes, and international art exhibits con-

The traditional Native American reverence for ancestors is displayed by members of Oklahoma's Comanche tribe, who demonstrate their support for laws prohibiting the desecration of sacred Indian burial sites in front of the Florida state capitol in 1990.

tinue to tell the stories inspired from the Wapapi, the priceless wampum story belts of the Great Wabenaki Confederacy
of Algonquian tribes native to New England and the Canadian coastal areas. When Tsonakwa's father "passed into the
spirit world," his mother gave him the beautiful handmade
boxes that held the tiny treasures he understood to be mne-
monics, or coded reminders. All of the stories, filled with
ancient histories and tribal energies, were contained in the
boxes. "When read like hieroglyphs, these things illustrate
the entire span of my father's life," writes Tsonakwa in
Shamanism, Magic, and the Busy Spider.

The books listed in the **Resources** section will allow you
to go ever deeper into your own special subject areas and
read about your tribe(s). Some of us have bloodlines from
more than one tribal group and region. Many tribal groups
suffered displacement and relocation, so yours will be an
often emotional research quest. Try to maintain an objective
balance as you look back across the pages of time. Yours is
a very special perspective, and you and your kinfolk are
notable survivors.

Resources

NATIVE AMERICAN TRIBES

Budak, Mike. *Grand Mound.* **Minnesota Historical Sites Series, no. 23. St. Paul: Minnesota Historical Society Press, 1995.**

> Dramatic glimpses into the ancient history of Woodland Indian peoples more than 2,500 years ago at this northern extent of our prehistoric Mound Builders' cultures.

Cash, Joseph H., and Hoover, Herbert T., eds. *To Be an Indian: An Oral History.* **St. Paul: Borealis Books, Minnesota Historical Society Press, 1995.**

> A collection of personal accounts of contemporary Northern Plains Indians from the Dakota, Lakota, and Winnebago communities.

Culin, Stewart. *Games of the North American Indians.* **New York: Dover Publications, 1975.**

> A large, valuable reference, with fine illustrations and excellent background details.

Densmore, Frances. *Chippewa Customs.* **St. Paul: Minnesota Historical Society Press, 1984.**

> A classic work, first published in 1929, recording early Chippewa (Ojibway) Indian lifeways and activities in the United States and Canada.

Downs, James F. *The Two Worlds of the Washo: An Indian Tribe of California and Nevada.* **Chicago: Holt, Rinehart and Winston, Inc., 1966.**

> This book chronicles the history, ecology, and adaptation to the "sad new world" of the nomadic households of the Washo people.

Dunn, Lynn P. *American Indians: A Study Guide and Source Book.* **Palo Alto, CA: R & E Research Associates, 1979.**

Cross-cultural study guide designed to give the teacher and student chronological facts. Extensive bibliographies.

Grobsmith, Elizabeth S. *Lakota of the Rosebud: A Contemporary Ethnography.* **Chicago: Holt, Rinehart and Winston, Inc., 1981.**

This contemporary study details how a complex reservation community adapts to modern culture. Fascinating and sensitive resource book.

Heizer, Robert F., ed. *Handbook of North American Indians, Vol. VIII: California.* **Washington, DC: Smithsonian Institution, 1978.**

This is perhaps the foremost scholarly work in this field, embracing the best of the earliest works and bringing together historical and prehistoric research.

Helm, June, ed. *Subarctic: Handbook of North American Indians, Vol. VI.* **Washington, DC: Smithsonian Institution, 1981.**

Impressive compilation of materials, covering the foremost research in this subject.

Hudson, Charles. *The Southeastern Indians.* **Knoxville: University of Tennessee Press, 1976.**

Scholarly presentation in more than 570 pages of the dynamic native cultures of our southeastern regions, from their earliest prehistory to recent times.

McFee, Malcolm. *Modern Blackfeet: Montanans on a Reservation.* **Prospect Heights, IL: Waveland Press, 1986.**

A sensitive study showing why assimilation has not completely occurred among the Blackfeet, and reflecting upon both Indian and white adaptations.

Reaman, G. Elmore. *The Trail of the Black Walnut,* **rev. ed. Baltimore: Genealogical Publishing Co., 1993.**

Superb research on the Pennsylvania German role in founding Upper Canada at the time of the American Revolution, when successive waves of "Plain Folk" (including Mennonites, Dunkers, Moravians, Amish, and Hutterites) migrated to Canada, taking numerous Native Americans along with them.

Rountree, Helen C. *Pocahontas' People: The Powhatan Indians of Virginia through Four Centuries.* **Civilization of the American Indian Series, vol. 196. Norman: University of Oklahoma Press, 1990.**

Outstanding scholarly treatment of the subject, with careful details and full resources.

———. *The Powhatan Indians of Virginia: Their Traditional Culture.* **Civilization of the American Indian Series, Vol. 193. Norman: University of Oklahoma Press, 1989.**

A definitive reference for this field.

Shadburn, Don L. *Cherokee Planters in Georgia 1832–1838.* **Pioneer-Cherokee Heritage Series, Vol. 2. Roswell, GA: Forsyth County Heritage Foundation, Historical Publications Division, 1989.**

This volume grew out of the author's larger work, *Unhallowed Intrusion: A Georgia Journal of Cherokee History and Genealogy,* and is an exhaustive study valuable to everyone interested in the region.

Stern, Theodore. *The Klamath Tribe: A People and Their Reservation.* **Seattle: University of Washington Press, 1966.**

Valuable descriptions of contemporary reservation life among the Klamath of Oregon, whose federal relations were terminated in 1954.

Vogel, Virgil J. *This Country Was Ours: A Documentary History of the American Indians*. New York: Harper & Row, 1972.

A sensitive, scholarly reference, filled with little-known details.

Warren, William W. *History of the Ojibway People*. St. Paul: Minnesota Historical Society Press, 1984.

A fascinating study written in 1852 by an author of Ojibway descent, based upon priceless oral histories. This is perhaps the most important history of the Ojibway ever written, according to most scholars.

Wolcott, Harry F. *A Kwakiutl Village and School (CSEC)*. Chicago: Holt, Rinehart and Winston, Inc., 1967.

A study of culture conflicts in this Northwest Coast native village.

NATIVE AMERICAN WOMEN

Allen, Paula Gunn, ed. *Grandmothers of the Light: A Medicine Woman's Source-Book*. Boston: Beacon Press, 1991.

Collections of goddess stories from across Native America, connecting the sacred and powerful relationships in our cultures and lives.

————. *Spider Woman's Granddaughters: Traditional Tales and Contemporary Writing by Native American Women*. New York: Fawcett Columbine Books, 1989.

Clear resonant voices of seventeen Native American women speak of the sacred traditions weaving together the rich fabrics of their tribal and spiritual identities.

Awiakta, Marilou. *Selu: Seeking the Corn-Mother's Wisdom*. Golden, CO: Fulcrum Publishing, 1993.

Spiritual tools for examining our lives, using Selu, the Cherokee Corn-Mother, as an enduring metaphor and reassuring guide and guardian, as we search more deeply for wisdom, understanding, and balance.

Bataille, Gretchen M., ed. *Native American Women: A Biographical Dictionary*. Garland Reference Library of the Social Sciences, Vol. 649. New York: Garland Publishing, 1993.

Native American women from diverse cultures and experiences are profiled. A valuable work.

————, and Sands, Kathleen M. *American Women Telling Their Lives*. Lincoln: University of Nebraska Press, 1984.

This careful work explores the fundamental nature of Native American societies, with perspectives on contemporary women's movements.

Niethammer, Carolyn. *Daughters of the Earth: The Lives of American Indian Women*. New York: Macmillan, Collier Books, 1977.

Descriptions of Native American women's lives, accomplishments, and legacies.

Perrone, Bobette; Stockel, H. Henrietta; and Krueger, Victoria. *Medicine Women, Curanderas, and Women Doctors*. Norman: University of Oklahoma Press, 1989.

A provocative book offering insight into the woman-centered healing systems of Native American cultures.

NATIVE AMERICANS THROUGHOUT HISTORY

Axtell, James. *The Invasion Within: The Contest of Cultures in Colonial America*. New York: Oxford University Press, 1985.

Contrasts English efforts to "civilize" Native Americans with the French willingness to accept their lifeways during the turbulent colonial struggles.

Ballantine, B., and Ballantine, I., eds. *The Native Americans: An Illustrated History*. Atlanta: Turner Publishing, 1993.

This massive volume spans thousands of generations from the Ice Age to the contemporary United States. Contributing scholars provide detailed native histories.

Bodmer, Karl; Thomas, Davis; and Ronnefeldt, Karin, eds. *People of the First Man: Life among the Plains Indians in Their Days of Glory: "The Firsthand Account of Prince Maximilian's Expedition up the Missouri River, 1833–1834."* New York: Dutton, 1976.

Second only to the Lewis and Clark Expedition journals some twenty years earlier, this large, beautiful book focuses on twenty-six Indian tribes. It has been hailed as a masterpiece of ethnographic reporting.

Debo, Angie. *A History of the Indians of the United States*. The Civilization of American Indian Series, Vol. 106. Norman: University of Oklahoma Press, 1989.

This in-depth historical survey includes Alaskan Aleut and Eskimo (Inuit and Inupiat) peoples. Well illustrated and carefully articulated by one of the finest scholars on the subject.

Dobyns, Henry F., and Swagerty, W. R. *Their Number Become Thinned: Native American Population Dy-*

namics in Eastern North America. Knoxville: University of Tennessee Press, 1983.

Foremost scholarly work on this subject, full of details.

Fiedel, Stuart J. *Prehistory of the Americas.* New York: Cambridge University Press, 1989.

A careful examination of Native American cultures before European contact.

Green, Barbara. "Virginia's Indians: Bridging the Centuries." *Virginia News Leader,* August, 1987.

A sensitive, careful examination of the remaining tribes in the Powhatan Confederacy in this region: the Chickahominy, Pamunkey, Mattaponi, Upper Mattaponi, Lumbee, Eastern Chickahominy, United Rappahannock, Nansemond, and Monacan.

Hudson, Charles. *The Southeastern Indians.* Knoxville: University of Tennessee Press, 1989.

Scholarly study by a noted authority on the rich culture of Native Americans in the southeastern United States.

Kopper, Philip. *The Smithsonian Book of North American Indians: Before the Coming of the Europeans.* Washington, DC: Smithsonian Institution Press, 1986.

Pre-Columbian America, with its diverse Native cultures, is carefully chronicled and beautifully illustrated.

Lewis, Thomas M. N., and Kneberg, Madeline. *Tribes that Slumber: Indians of the Tennessee Region.* Knoxville: University of Tennessee Press, 1986.

Detailed focus on the "Principal People" (the Cherokee) from earliest prehistory onward.

National Geographic Society Staff. *The World of the American Indian.* Washington, DC: National Geographic Society, 1974.

Foremost Native American scholars write about their heritage in this beautifully illustrated and deeply felt resource.

Nichols, Roger I. *The American Indian: Past and Present.* **3d ed. New York: Knopf, 1986.**

Valuable essays illuminating many aspects of Indian America through diverse voices.

Perdue, Theda. *Native Carolinians: The Indians of North Carolina.* **Raleigh: North Carolina Department of Cultural Resources, Division of Archives and History, 1985.**

Outstanding small reference book, with scholarly data and fine illustrations.

Sando, Joe S. *Pueblo Nations: Eight Centuries of Pueblo Indian History.* **Sante Fe: Clear Light Publishers, 1994.**

A clear, valuable synthesis by a noted Jemez Pueblo writer and historian. Brings the nineteen pueblos in New Mexico to new light and life in sensitive, perceptive prose, with photographs and maps.

Sattler, Helen Roney. *The Earliest Americans.* **New York: Clarion Books, 1993.**

From earliest evidence of human migrations to the Americas, to detailed early cultural settlements, this well-illustrated, clear text traces the history of the first Americans.

Simmons, William S. *The Narragansett.* **New York: Chelsea House, 1989.**

Native Algonquians, who lived in what is now Rhode Island, played key roles in the settlement history of the Northeast and continue to exert dynamic influences. This is one volume of an extensive series by noted contemporary scholars, "Indians of North America," which profiles most individual tribes and major subject areas such as *Women in American Indian Society; Urban Indians; Ameri-*

can *Indian Literature; Federal Indian Policy; The Archaeology of North America.*

Super, John C. *Food, Conquest, and Colonization in Sixteenth-Century Spanish America.* **Albuquerque: University of New Mexico Press, 1988.**

Native history viewed through the special lens of food.

Taylor, C. F., and Sturtevant, W. C., eds. *The Native Americans: The Indigenous People of North America.* **New York: Smithmark Publishers, Salamander Books, 1991.**

A careful examination of Native American history in nine cultures. Detailed ethnographic objects and archival photographs.

Thornton, Russell. *American Indian Holocaust and Survival: A Population History Since 1492.* **The Civilization of the American Indian Series, Vol. 186. Norman: University of Oklahoma Press, 1987.**

Valuable scholarly perspectives address this wide-ranging subject, with a stunning overview of North American Indian history.

Viola, Herman J. *After Columbus: The Smithsonian Chronicle of North American Indians.* **Washington, DC: Smithsonian Institution Press, 1990.**

Traditional cultures and countless legacies are carefully described and beautifully photographed.

Woodward, Grace Steele. *Pocahontas.* **Norman: University of Oklahoma Press, 1969.**

Excellent early study with fine illustrations.

NATIVE AMERICAN CULTURE AND TRADITIONS

Beck, Peggy; Walters, Anna Lee; and Francisco, Nia. *The Sacred: Ways of Knowledge, Sources of Life.*

Tsaile, AZ: Navajo Community College Press, and Flagstaff, AZ: Northland Publishing Co., 1990.

A compelling guide to those who wish to explore Native American spirituality.

Deloria, Vine, Jr. *Custer Died for Our Sins: An Indian Manifesto*. New York: Macmillan, 1969.

In a unique study written with acerbic humor, this acclaimed Native American author explodes the old myths and stereotypes so harmful to contemporary Native American dignity and achievements.

Eastman, Charles Alexander. *The Soul of the Indian: An Interpretation*. Lincoln: University of Nebraska Press, 1980.

Charles Eastman (1858–1939) was a noted doctor of Sioux descent who devoted his life to helping his fellow Native Americans preserve their lifeways while adapting to the white world. This is one of three books he wrote during his complex, fascinating life.

Fitzhugh, William W., and Crowell, Aron. *Crossroads of Continents: Cultures of Siberia and Alaska*. Washington, DC: Smithsonian Institution Press, 1988.

Rich trove of artifacts, cultural histories, and prehistories from the northern regions where two great continents meet. Detailed and illustrated exhibition catalog.

Lindquist, Mark A., and Zanger, Martin, eds. *Buried Roots and Indestructible Seeds: The Survival of American Indian Life in Story, History, and Spirit*. Madison: University of Wisconsin Press, 1993.

Anthology highlighting central values and traditions in various Native American societies.

Peters, Russell M. *Clambake: A Wampanoag Tradition*. We Are Still Here Series: Native Americans Today. Minneapolis: Lerner Publications, 1992.

Detailed look at the East Coast clambake as celebrated by the Wampanoag People in Mashpee, Massachusetts, on Cape Cod. Photographed by John Madama.

Trimble, Stephen. *The People: Indians of the American Southwest*. Sante Fe: School of American Research Press, 1993.

An in-depth, sensitive introduction to fifty modern Indian Nations throughout the American Southwest, accompanied by the author's photographs.

Weinstein, Laurie, ed. *Enduring Traditions: The Native Peoples of New England*. Westport, CT: Greenwood Press, 1994.

Essays on important aspects of Native Algonquian tribes in the Northeast and their influences on our collective history.

Wilson, Gilbert L. *Buffalo Bird Woman's Garden: Agriculture of the Hidatsa Indians*. St. Paul: Minnesota Historical Society Press, 1987.

Classic study in this field, well illustrated, touching on many areas of family and history beyond agriculture.

Yoder, Carolyn P., ed. "The Cultures of Pre-Columbian North America." *History Magazine for Young People*, Vol. 14, 1993.

Features selected cultures, with insights on a vital period of ancient America.

LEGAL AND POLITICAL ISSUES

Clark, Blue. *Lone Wolf v. Hitchcock: Treaty Rights and Indian Law at the End of the Nineteenth Century*. Lincoln: University of Nebraska Press and Bison Books, 1994.

This landmark case of 1903 violated the treaty and lands belonging to individual tribes, especially the Kiowa, and charts their struggles to cope with society's pressures, attitudes, and economic system.

Cohen, Felix. *Handbook of Federal Indian Law.* **Albuquerque: University of New Mexico Press, 1942.**

Consult the foremost reference work in this field to gain a broad base of understanding.

Deloria, Vine, Jr. *Behind the Trail of Broken Treaties: An Indian Declaration of Independence.* **New York: Dell Delta Books, 1981.**

The author, an attorney, is a leading Native American (Sioux) spokesman and crusader for government respect for Native American people and their treaties. He argues that Congress should define the Indian tribes as small nations under the protection of the United States, recognizing their inherent right to political and cultural existence.

————, and Lytle, Clifford M. *American Indians, American Justice.* **Austin: University of Texas Press, 1983.**

Two attorneys explore the complexities of the current status of Native American legal and political rights.

Echo-Hawk, Roger C., and Echo-Hawk, Walter R. *Battlefields and Burial Grounds: The Indian Struggle to Protect Ancestral Graves in the United States.* **Minneapolis: Lerner Publications, 1994.**

Pawnee attorney and Pawnee historian (brothers) team up to describe the Native Americans' struggle to reclaim and rebury their dead. They worked for the American Indian Religious Freedom Act of 1978 and the Native American Graves Protection and Repatriation Act of 1990.

Filler, Louis, and Guttman, Allen, eds. *The Removal of the Cherokee Nation: Manifest Destiny or National*

Dishonor? Huntington, NY: Robert E. Krieger Publishing Co., 1977.

Unique series of essays addressing a shameful period in U.S. history.

Grinde, Donald A., Jr. *The Iroquois and the Founding of the American Nation.* San Francisco: American Indian Historian Press, 1977.

Scholarly detailed accounts of Native American concepts of governing and representation of the people.

Horsman, Reginald. *Expansion and American Indian Policy, 1783–1812.* Norman: University of Oklahoma Press, 1992.

Valuable examination of a critical period in native policy-making.

Jennings, Francis. *The Invasion of America: Indians, Colonialism, and the Cant of Conquest.* Chapel Hill: University of North Carolina Press, 1975.

Major study in this field by a noted scholar. Grasp the range of our history and the mindset which continues to shape much of life today.

Lawson, Michael L. *Dammed Indians: The Pick-Sloan Plan and the Missouri River Sioux, 1944–1980.* Foreword by Vine Deloria, Jr. Norman: University of Oklahoma Press, 1982.

Lawson examines this plan and the subsequent development in the Missouri River Basin, which flooded more than 202,000 acres of fine Sioux bottomland.

Lyons, Oren; Mohawk, John; Deloria, Vine, Jr., and others. *Exiled in the Land of the Free: Democracy,*

Indian Nations, and the U.S. Constitution. **Sante Fe: Clear Light Publishers, 1993.**

Impressive essays by eight Native American leaders and scholars presenting strong cases for Native American sovereignty.

Chapter 5
Tracing Your Family Tree

Who Is American Indian?

"American Indian" emerged as an ethnic category during the period of European settlement. Native peoples had their own names for themselves, which usually translated to "the people," "real people," "true people," or people of a particular place. The Abenaki are "people of the dawn." The Alabama translates to "plant gatherers," and the Aleut means "islanders." Assiniboine are "those who cook with stones," and Catawba are "people of the river." Cayuga means "people of the marsh," and Erie means "wild cats" or "nation of the cat." Native names still have much to tell us about our origins. Tribal names, as we see here, are often the people's names for themselves. Sometimes the tribal name that sticks is one given by enemies, allies, or the early European trappers and traders who first encountered the tribe.

For example, some tribes today bear names given to them by their enemies, because of their fierceness, like the Iroquois (which is an Algonquian term meaning "real adders" or "poisonous snakes"), and Mohawk (an Algonquian term of fear meaning "cannibals" or "wolves"). The Iroquois call themselves the Haudenosaunee ("people of the longhouse"), and the Mohawk call themselves Ganiengehaka ("people of the flint country"), the keepers of the eastern door for the Six Nations of the Iroquois League.

Christopher Columbus called the Taino people he first encountered in 1492 *una gente en dios*, "a people living in God." In earliest Spanish texts all native people of the New World became Indios, and then Indians.

While there are still many fullbloods in many tribes, centuries of intermarriage between tribes and marriages with

African, Asian, and Anglo spouses have clouded the defini-
tion of who is Indian. Along the Atlantic Coast during the
colonial period, English, Spanish, French, German, Irish,
Portugese, African, Italian, and Dutch intermarriages with
Indians were not uncommon.

Indian ethnicity is a multi-faceted, complex issue. According to the 1990 U.S. Census, almost 2 million Americans
described themselves as Indian. Each tribe has its own regulations that determine who is considered a member of the
tribe. These guidelines are occasionally modified and up-
dated depending upon a tribe's special needs. The degree
of Indian blood one can claim is often a factor in determining tribal membership.

Usually at least one parent must qualify as a tribal member for the children to become members. In some tribes
members must be able to prove their descent from one of
the tribe's matriarchs, or Elder Women. Other tribes require
bilateral descent through both parents. Tribal recognition
is necessary for federal recognition, yet not all tribes are
federally recognized. Over 300 tribes have federal recognition; the majority of these are west of the Mississippi. In
addition, more than 200 Alaskan villages have been federally
recognized. All of these exist as unique political entities
functioning within their state and federal systems. Federally
recognized tribes are allowed to govern their own members.

Many other tribes exist with their own particular struc-
tures, and some are incorporated within their state legal
systems. Some reservations in California are called
rancherias, and most Alaskan villages are known as Native
Villages. The 14-million-acre Navajo Reservation is the
largest reservation in the United States, located in the famous Four Corners region of the Southwest—embracing
much of northern Arizona, and corners of New Mexico,
Utah, and Colorado. The smallest is the Golden Hill
Paugussett Reservation in Trumbull, Connecticut, which is
only one-quarter of an acre: one house for one family, whit-
tled away from a larger land-holding. It is the oldest reservation in the country, established in 1659.

Members of the Penobscot tribe of Maine were among the beneficiaries of legal action in the 1970s that attempted to compensate Native Americans for injustices they had endured at the hands of the U.S. government. Above, a Penobscot chief posed with his wife, daughter, and grandchild in 1920.

The Indian Reorganization Act of 1934, followed by decisions of the Indian Claims Commission, accelerated the need for careful determination of Indian identity. While there are more than 300 federally recognized tribes in the United States, perhaps another 200 American Indian groups and tribes with bylaws and constitutions have the potential to be federally recognized. The Indian Reorganization Act (or the Wheeler-Howard Act) in 1934, under the more progressive government of President Franklin D. Roosevelt and the Commissioner of Indian Affairs, John Collier, reversed decades of harmful assimilation and allotment practices intended to "civilize" native people while suppressing their cultures and stealing their lands. The ramifications of the 1934 act were noteworthy. Yet the federal government continued to hold unilateral powers over Indian tribes, and after another decade many of Collier's better policies were reversed by a new wave of federal assimilation policies. These echoed the tactics used by early missionaries, educators, and overseers, who worked to acculturate, assimilate, detribalize, and "Americanize" the indigenous peoples on the grounds that this would make them "better" and more self-sufficient.

The Indian Claims Commission, established in 1946 for tribes to file their long-standing grievances for broken treaties and stolen lands, and through which they might seek legal land claims and receive monetary compensation, actually worked against them, often resulting in terminations of these claims. From 1954 to 1962 Congress terminated its federal trust relationship with sixty-one tribes and bands, pushing them further into financial despair. Additional deceit was practiced in collusion with white economic interests—as among the Menominee of Wisconsin, who were terminated (federal services and protection were withdrawn) while rich timber concerns and their allies in Congress acquired the tribe's land-based resources.

Because of changing federal policies toward Native Americans, your tribe may no longer possess its own land or enjoy protected status. Learning about the specific history of your tribe, and drawing conclusions about how government policies affected your ancestors, may become an important part of your family history research.

Filling in Your Family Tree

As you continue to trace your own family tree, filling in the branches and twigs that you find among your kinfolk, make a note of all vital information you find for each individual. On your family tree, which can be a chart or drawing, place directly below each name the person's birth date and place, death date and place (if appropriate); and where he or she was married. Some people also like to add the age of each relative, the number of children born into each marriage, and causes of death. This format gives you, at a glance, very valuable family data. The addition of details such as longevity records, family sizes, and even occupations makes your family tree much more personal and informative. How many ironworkers, mechanics, farmers, and midwives were in your mother's line? Were there any herbalists, healers, artists, or doctors in your father's line? Do you see occupational or health patterns in your family tree? Chances are that you will discover some fascinating patterns as you accumulate more data. Are your parents both from the same reservation? Are they from different tribes, or different ethnic backgrounds? As you pull together the pieces of information and answer these questions, you are tracing your family tree and developing your family genealogy. This is some of the information you will need if you are interested in applying for tribal enrollment and membership.

Remember, however, that "reaching for your roots" and doing family history research is a great deal more than names on a page with pertinent dates and facts. And being Native American is a great deal more than having a tribal enrollment card.

Family and Tribal Membership

It is important to make the distinction between general Indian ancestry and specific tribal descent. Usually, a person may not be an official member of more than one tribe. For instance, if a Connecticut Mohegan man marries a Navajo woman, they may choose to register all of their children on the Navajo tribal rolls in Arizona, although they continue to live and work in Connecticut. With the Navajo, as with many American Indian tribes, descent traditionally passes through the mother's lineage.

Most tribes have membership committees and tribal historians to determine eligibility for membership and resolve disputes. If you are accepted as an official member of the tribe, you will probably be issued a card confirming that. The *Handbook of Federal Indian Law* notes, "Tribal membership as determined by the Indian tribe or community itself is often an essential element. In fact, a person of complete Indian ancestry who has never had relations with any Indian tribe may be considered a non-Indian for some legal

There are more than 540 Native American tribes, and over 300 of them have federal recognition. Members of the Zuni tribe are pictured in this photograph from the late 1800s.

purposes." There are many areas in our country where Native Americans, even fullbloods, may choose to live apart from their tribes.

There were many dark years for Native American people when it was not acceptable in American society to be Indian. As a result, many families lived for generations in denial of their heritage. Many feel the discrimination so painfully that they still choose not to acknowledge their Indian blood. Even within the same family, not everyone wants to celebrate being Indian.

Your search may be clouded by these and many more sensitive issues, including some that family members may not be willing to discuss. Some families bear scars from psychological pain for many generations without realizing or acknowledging that problems exist.

Be sensitive and careful. Always be respectful of the feelings of family members. Be persistent, but don't push too hard. Do not press relatives for information they seem unwilling to provide.

Tribal Enrollment

Each tribe has its own criteria for enrollment. "Membership requirements often involve blood quantum, lineage, enrollment or allotment status, and residence. Many tribes do not require a minimum blood quantum: one often has to trace only lineage to earlier tribal members at points in history," according to Russell Thornton.★ To find out the requirements for your tribe, write to the tribal headquarters and request this information and any other available data, such as tribal ordinances regarding enrollment. Cecelie Svinth Carpenter, in *How to Research American Indian Blood Lines*, suggests that you write to the nearest office of the Bureau of Indian Affairs for the information if you do not get a response from the tribe in a reasonable length of time.

★Thornton, Russell. *American Indian Holocaust and Survival* (Norman: University of Oklahoma Press, 1987).

Patience is necessary for this process because a tribal council may consider enrollment annually, or only at certain times.

Allotment has come to mean the suppression of Indian cultures. Congress passed the Dawes General Allotment Act in 1887. This concept broke up the land of Indian reservations, allotting 160-acre parcels to heads of Indian families, assuming that it would be economically used or farmed, and surplus Indian lands were given to non-Indians for full use. Unfortunately, the result of the allotment system was that Indians often rented or sold their land and thereby lost their holdings. Tribes also lost many acres. The allotment system was ended by law in 1934.

Many more people are now seeking tribal enrollment. Enrollment may bring certain benefits, whether you live on or off a reservation. Enrollment in federally recognized tribes usually makes one eligible for educational assistance, health care, and some hunting, fishing, or income rights, depending on the tribe.

Certificate Document of Indian Blood (CDIB)

To obtain a CDIB card you must meet the established requirements for tribal enrollment, generally by showing the degree of Indian blood in your ancestry. Check with your tribe for their specific requirements. Generally, you can hold only one tribal membership. The Certificate Document of Indian Blood is a little card that resembles a driver's license. Some contain a tiny picture of the holder and the official tribal stamp. It is an important document of tribal membership and is especially useful for artists and craftsmen who want to be considered for membership or acceptance in special organizations, such as Native American art shows and powwows.

If your family bloodlines descend from the Cherokee, Creek, and Powhatan peoples, you need to decide which one of these is your strongest descent line, and trace this line as far back as you can. It is possible that these descent bloodlines are too intermingled or distant to qualify you for membership in any one tribe.

Enrichment comes in many forms. You will probably never know all the details about your ancestors, but tracing your roots and appreciating all of your bloodlines will still be exciting and interesting. Do not consider your search a "failure" simply because you have not gained tribal enrollment. There are many other rewards of family history research.

You may be on a personal quest to learn more about yourself. By honoring your family, and their families, going back through time, you may find that your search helps to fill in some blank spaces on your family tree. Perhaps those spaces are filled with Indian heritage. Or perhaps the root and origin of specific Indian blood cannot be determined. Some of us meet many roadblocks, and we become aware of more barriers as we try to progress. Persevere. There are many avenues of help, and when one path seems blocked, there are always others. Perhaps the ideas and resources in this book will help to guide you along your path.

Folklore and Oral History

"When we were young it was our grandmother who gathered us around to tell us of many things: of how the world began; of where we came from; why we must respect all living things; of the wonders of the universe. She always told us of the old ways. And when we were told these things, these truths, we searched her face of many wrinkles and believed she must have been there, way back then, in the beginning—so vivid were her words and the pictures she created in our mind's eye. It was only when we were much older that we realized that this was the way of the elders. These words were the traditions being passed down from their grandmothers and grandfathers."

—Trudie Lamb Richmond, Schaghticoke historian, elder, and assistant director of the Institute for American Indian Studies, Washington, Connecticut

Colorful legacies of family folklore swirl through all families. Sometimes the folklore grows up around myths, changing facts to relieve personal pain and to whitewash areas of a past marked by discrimination and ostracism. Sadly, in some families, Indian relatives have been whitewashed right out of existence. In many families the "truths" were carefully and firmly hidden in order to prevent discrimination, and sometimes to enable the children to go to normal schools, which would have been forbidden under the segregation laws in many states. Indians, being "people of color," suffered many problems of discrimination.

Sometimes the family folklore is fairly accurate, though, and can help you fill in gaps in information. When the information flow stops or slows down, it is a good idea to relax and collect folklore. One way to gather stories about your family is through interviews. Who is better qualified to tell you about your family history than the family members themselves? Of course, you must always confirm any oral history you gather in interviews with vital records and documents.

Perhaps your quest for your family roots began with a few simple questions, and once those were answered a whole set of new questions cropped up. List your questions, in their order of priority to you, and make a simple questionnaire that you can copy and give (or send) to several key relatives. Ask them to answer what they can and send the details back to you. You might offer to share fuller details of your work as it grows.

Some important questions to ask are:
- Where are the family photos kept? Are there family albums?
- Are there family documents and papers, letters and postcards?
- Is there a family Bible or record book?
- Are there family samplers, quilts, or other memorabilia?
- What are some favorite family foods and recipes?
- Who recalls the old family stories? Are any written down?

Once you have gathered some basic information, you will want to probe further. Keep a special notebook for oral history interviews. You might be interested in topics such as

A Native American woman watches over her grandchildren in 1944. Storytelling is a traditional Native American method of passing down wisdom through the generations. Your own elders may be valuable sources of family lore.

where your interviewee grew up and his or her memories of that place, relationships with family members, occupation, and other interests.

To what extent has your interviewee retained aspects of his or her Native American heritage? Does he or she participate in any Native American festivals, dances, celebrations, or religious ceremonies? Does he or she enjoy cooking and eating Native American foods?

Ask your interviewee to confirm basic facts about his or her life and about the lives of relatives he or she knew well. If, for example, your great-grandmother is no longer alive, your grandmother may be able to help you narrow down when and where she was born, married, and died. If you have an idea of the year and the location in which events occurred, it will be much easier to do your own research.

Make a family chart based upon the information you have gathered, and give copies to family members who might be willing to check it for you. Another interesting project might be to make a map showing family movement and migration patterns. Your family map and migration diagram might begin with tracing a map of the United States or North America. Some of us need a world map, including Europe, Africa, or Asia. You may also want to trace a map of one region or state and show your family's movements over several generations. Perhaps your kinfolk have always lived in one region. As you look over the brief face of history, you will realize how rare it is to be able to remain in one place. Take your map along to interviews and ask if your inter- viewee has anything to add to it.

If you have access to a tape recorder, and if your relatives do not object, it is very useful to tape-record interviews. You may even want to videotape them if you have access to the equipment. This can turn your family history project into a vibrant, living document to be enjoyed by all family mem- bers. If you tape-record interviews, be sure to take notes at the same time. Jot down important points so that you will know what to listen for when you transcribe the tape. Tak- ing notes may also help you come up with new questions.

If your relatives live far away, you can still interview them without making expensive long-distance phone calls. Put your questions into the form of a questionnaire and send them to your relatives, along with a polite letter telling them about your project and asking them for help. Include a stamped, self-addressed envelope so they have no excuse not to reply!

A Native American Photo Album

Locations of major North American Indian tribes through the earliest period of European settlement (early 1600s). Some tribes have remained in these original areas, while others have dispersed.

Native Americans—also called North American Indians—were the first peoples to inhabit the American continent. They crossed a land bridge from Siberia to Alaska, possibly as early as 40,000 BC. Did the vast variety of distinct Native American peoples develop after the first peoples migrated from Asia? Or were the migrants themselves already divided into different cultural groups? Anthropologists are still struggling with these questions. What we do know is that Native Americans, with ingenuity and determination, found amazing and creative ways to live in the Americas: through hunting, plant cultivation, and utilizing all the resources available to them. They developed unique and complex societies long before their first contact with Europeans. We still have much to learn from their traditional ways of living. Recent years have seen a resurgent interest in Native American achievements in art, crafts, folklore, cooking, medicine, and many other endeavors. But we can take our greatest lessons from the triumph of the Native American spirit in the face of disease, forced migrations, military takeover, discrimination, racism, and other threats that have plagued them since the first arrival of Europeans on their land. Native American leaders of today have inherited a legacy of strength and dignity from their predecessors—leaders such as Chief Joseph, Black Elk, Crazy Horse, and Geronimo—who refused to stand by and allow their lands and peoples to be destroyed.

This painting by Benjamin West depicts the signing of the celebrated treaty of 1682 between William Penn, the English Quaker and founder of Pennsylvania, and Tamenend, leader of the Delaware people. Despite Penn's goodwill toward the Delawares and his hopes for longstanding peace between whites and Native Americans, the influx of white settlers quickly displaced the Delawares and other Native American groups not long after Penn's death in 1718.

Lacrosse was invented by Native Americans and was used in some tribes as a war training exercise. Originally called *baggataway,* this sport was a violent game with few fixed rules. French settlers adopted *baggataway* and popularized it among Europeans. It is from the French that it received its current name. Lacrosse continues to be a popular team sport in the United States today.

The Tlingit are a Native American tribe who live on the Pacific coast of southeastern Alaska and northwestern Canada. They rely on fishing for survival. The Tlingit are known for their skill in wood carving, exemplified by this Tlingit Bear Chief's clan hat.

Dancing continues to be a central part of life for many North American Indians. Traditional dances are a major event at intertribal powwows in the United States and Canada. Above, boys from the Warm Springs Indian tribe dance to the beat of their tribal elders' drums in The Dalles, Oregon.

The Pueblo peoples, including the Zuni and the Hopi, live in the southwestern United States and
number some 40,000. Many Pueblo people maintain the traditions and way of life of their ancestors.
Agriculture and pottery are still their principal ways of earning a livelihood. This woman is dressed for
a ceremonial dance at the San Ildefonso pueblo in western New Mexico.

The Pueblo peoples are the modern descendants of the Anasazi, an ancient civilization that inhabited the Four Corners area, where Colorado, Utah, New Mexico, and Arizona meet, between 500 and 1600 AD. The term "pueblo" refers not only to the group of people, but to their style of housing as well. The Pueblo learned their building technique—multi-level dwelling complexes made of mud and stone—from their Anasazi ancestors. Above are the ruins of an Anasazi pueblo in the Chaco Culture National Historical Park in New Mexico.

Four generations of the Smith/Hamilton family gather after a special dinner at the Pawnee Senior Citizen Center at tribal headquarters in Pawnee, Oklahoma. At one time the Pawnee lived in Nebraska, but they were forced to cede their land to the U.S. government in 1876. Social centers are important to some contemporary Native American groups, as they provide the people with a solid social base in the absence of a strong geographic one.

Many Native Americans practice the arts and crafts of their ancestors, either for practical use or for sale and display. Above, two Mohawk sisters from Akwesasne, the St. Regis Reservation in upstate New York and Canada, practice traditional crafts. Irene Richmond (left) weaves black ash splint baskets, and her sister, Sara Ransom, plaits sweetgrass braids.

Leonard Crow Dog is a Lakota Sioux spiritual leader and medicine man. Born on the Rosebud
Reservation in South Dakota, Crow Dog has been one of the primary leaders of the Native
American civil rights movement. He was involved in the revival of the Ghost Dance at the Siege
of Wounded Knee in 1973, when Native American activists siezed and held the historic
hamlet for seventy-one days. The Ghost Dance is a sacred dance that prophesies the return of
American land to its original Indian inhabitants. The dance was outlawed by the
U.S. government in 1891.

In August of 1990, David Hill of the Choctaw tribe led a group of Native Americans to Seattle, Washington. The "Longest Ride," as it came to be known, was meant to call attention to issues of environmental, constitutional, treaty, and human rights. It was specifically intended to draw attention to the cause of imprisoned Native American activist Leonard Peltier, who was convicted of killing an FBI agent in 1975. Many believe that Peltier did not receive a fair trial.

In anticipation of the 500th anniversary of Christopher Columbus's arrival in North America, many people chose to view Columbus Day from a different perspective, one that took into account the legacy of destruction of Native American peoples. The result was the first Indigenous Peoples Day. Native Americans from across the country came to Berkeley, California, to participate in this all-day event.

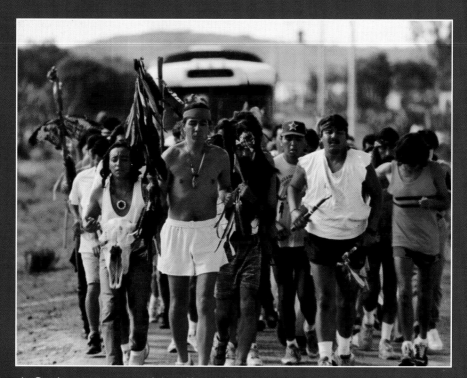

In October, 1992, a group of about fifty mostly North American Indian people participated in a run from the United States to the pyramids of Teotihuacan in Mexico. The runners, who came from as far north as Alaska, were met at Teotihuacan's Pyramid of the Sun by a group of runners from South America. The run was in protest of the 500th anniversary of Columbus's landing in the Americas.

Ben Nighthorse Campbell of Colorado was the first Native American to be elected to the U.S. Senate. A 1982 inductee into the Council of 44 Chiefs in the Northern Cheyenne Indian tribe, Senator Campbell is the chairman of the Senate Subcommittee on Parks, Historic Preservation, and Recreation and a member of the Senate Committee on Indian Affairs. Here, Senator Campbell and Senator Carol Moseley Braun share a laugh before posing for a portrait with other Senate newcomers on November 9, 1992.

In 1985, Wilma Mankiller was elected chief of the Cherokee Nation, the second-largest Native American tribe in the United States. Mankiller was the first woman ever to achieve this distinguished position, and she repeated that feat in 1987 when she won reelection. Above, Mankiller meets with President Clinton and Gaiashkibos, chairman of the Lac Courte Oreilles Chippewa, at the White House in 1994.

Wes Studi (right) talks with Julius "Josh" Drum during the Totem Awards ceremony in Beverly Hills, California, on February 6, 1993. The awards honor Native Americans for their achievements in and contributions to the entertainment industry. Studi received an award for outstanding performance in a film for his portrayal of Magua in *The Last of the Mohicans*. Drum was honored as outstanding new performer for his work in *Thunderheart*.

Family Reunions

Family reunions are great occasions to conduct interviews and collect folklore and oral history. These events are so vital that many families advertise the dates and times in order to get more family members to come and share their interests and information. Numerous historical and genealogical publications and Native American newspapers list upcoming family reunions. Family historians come to these events with questionnaires and genealogical forms.

Resources

GENEALOGY BASICS

Baselt, Fonda D. *Sunny Side of Genealogy*. **Baltimore: Genealogical Publishing Co., 1988.**

A delightfully comic look at the subject.

Baxter, Angus. *Do's and Don'ts for Ancestor Hunters*. **Baltimore: Genealogical Publishing Co., 1988.**

Inspirational, timely advice from a celebrated genealogist with more than forty years of experience.

————. *In Search of Your Canadian Roots*, **rev. ed. Baltimore: Genealogical Publishing Co., 1994.**

Step-by-step guide to the records and record repositories in each of the eleven provinces, the Yukon, and the Northwest Territories, and how to use these data to build a family tree or write a family history.

Beard, Timothy Field, with Denise Demong. *How to Find Your Family Roots*. **New York: McGraw-Hill, 1977.**

More than 1,000 pages of data and resources by one of the foremost librarians and genealogists in the field. Especially valuable Native American resources.

Bennett, Archibald. *Finding Your Forefathers in America*. **Salt Lake City: Bookcraft, 1957.**

This old but valuable resource contains an especially useful chapter on Pocahontas and her descendants.

Cerny, Johni, and Eakle, Arlene, eds. *The Source: A Guidebook of American Genealogy*. **Salt Lake City: Ancestry, Inc., 1985.**

Excellent resource guide. See especially chapter 17, by George J. Nixon, on "Records Relating to Native American Research: The Five Civilized Tribes."

Everton, George B., Jr. *The Handy Book for Genealogists.* **8th ed. Logan, UT: Everton Publishers, 1991.**

Each state is listed with a brief review of its history, counties, printed sources relating to that state, archives, libraries, and genealogical societies with addresses.

Greenwood, Val D. *The Researcher's Guide to American Genealogy.* **2d ed. Baltimore: Genealogical Publishing Co., 1990.**

One of the best books on the subject, covering the principles and details of genealogical research and the various classes of records used.

Gunderson, Ted L. *How to Locate Anyone Anywhere Without Leaving Home.* **New York: E. P. Dutton, 1989.**

Guide to finding addresses for a living person in the United States. This may be useful for tracking down hard-to-find family members.

Johnson, Richard S. *How to Locate Anyone Who Has Been in the Military: Armed Forces Locator Directory.* **5th ed. Burlington, NC: MIE Publishing, 1993.**

Valuable reference for help in locating relatives who have served in the armed services.

Jones, Henry Z. *Psychic Roots: Serendipity and Intuition in Genealogy.* **Baltimore: Genealogical Publishing Co., 1995.**

This well-researched book by a highly esteemed genealogist shows how to use coincidence and intuition to your advantage.

Krause, Carol. *How Healthy Is Your Family Tree?: A Complete Guide to Tracing Your Family's Medical* *and Behavioral History*. New York: Doubleday Book of the Month Club, 1992.

> A user-friendly workbook to show you how to collect the facts, then use that knowledge to prevent illness and destructive behaviors.

Nankin, Frances, ed. "Genealogy: A Personal History." *Cobblestone*, November, 1980.

> Valuable preliminary "how-to" guide with helpful details and inspirations. Written especially for young readers.

Stryker-Rodda, Harriet. *How to Climb Your Family Tree: Genealogy for Beginners*. Baltimore: Genealogical Publishing Co., 1992.

> This entertaining, user-friendly guide shows you how to start your research and find clues in family memorabilia.

Westin, Jeane Eddy. *Finding Your Roots: How Every American Can Trace His Ancestors—At Home and Abroad*. New York: Ballantine Books, 1989.

> This detailed resource book guides you skillfully through the many genealogical resources available. Includes specific information on Native American genealogy.

ORAL HISTORY AND TRADITIONS

Arthur, Stephen, and Arthur, Julia. *Your Life and Times*. Baltimore: Genealogical Publishing Co., 1994.

> An oral history guide in fifty pages, this handbook takes you step by step through the process of taping the vital details of your life.

Barrett, Samuel A., ed. *Pomo Myths*. Milwaukee: Milwaukee Public Museum, 1993.

> This huge study delves deeply into the Pomo stories and tribal customs recorded in 1914–15 in California. The

stories begin in the time when supernatural beings inhabited the earth, before the creation of the present race of human beings. Transformation and trickster tales abound, like "Sapsucker Tricks Coyote in Hair-Dressing" and "The Rescue from Growing Rock by Measuring Worm."

Bayliss, Clara. *A Treasury of Eskimo Tales*. **New York: Crowell, 1922.**

Eleven stories from the central Eskimo, embellished with the supernatural. The Bering Strait tales of Raven the Creator ring with considerable poetic wisdom.

Bell, Corydon. *John Rattling-Gourd of Bid Cove, A Collection of Cherokee Indian Legends*. **New York: Macmillan, 1955.**

In these twenty-four "how and why" stories from the elders on the Qualla Indian Reservation in Cherokee, North Carolina, we see the everyday relationships of young people to nature.

Boas, Franz, ed. *Bella Bella Tales*. **New York: American Folklore Society, G. E. Stechert, 1932.**

Characteristic elements of Northwest Coast cultures are displayed in these raven stories, ancestor tales, and tales of encounters with supernatural beings, especially the "Cannibal-of-the-North-End-of-the-World."

———. *Kwakiutl Tales*. **New York: Columbia University Press, 1935–43.**

Collected during the winter of 1930–31 on the Northwest Coast by one of the major North American anthropologists and ethnologists, these trickster and transformer tales are concerned with many of life's unexplainables. Ghosts and dwarfs also enrich the colorful fabric of this landmark work.

Caswell, Helen R. *Shadows from the Singing House: Eskimo Folk Tales*. **Rutland, VT: C. E. Tuttle Co., 1968.**

> Soft-pencil illustrations by Robert Mayokok, an Eskimo artist, enrich this "song" narrative of eighteen stories, including the Sedna myth, a Tsimshian Indian raven tale, and Eskimo tales of monsters and supernatural beings.

Clay, Charles. *Swampy Cree Legends*. **Toronto: Macmillan, 1938.**

> Northern Manitoba Swampy Cree legends as narrated by a Native American grandmother, Kuskapatchees, "The Smoky One," a gifted storyteller who weaves a spell about Wesukechak, the trickster hero.

Curry, Jane L. *Down from the Lonely Mountain: California Indian Tales*. **New York: Harcourt, Brace & World, 1965.**

> Beautifully illustrated retellings of twelve tales from the "time when the world was new and the animals helped to shape it." Blue Jay, Crow, Fox, and Coyote play wicked parts along with the Wind People, Thunder, and his daughters Churning Cloud, Heavy Rain, Storm Ice, and Swift-as-Lightning.

Cushing, Frank H. *Zuni Breadstuff*. **New York: Museum of the American Indian, Heye Foundation, 1920.**

> A classic collection of myths, ceremonies, and daily customs relating to corn by a white man who lived with the Zuni from 1879 to 1884.

Dorsey, George A. *Traditions of the Skidi Pawnee*. **Boston: Houghton Mifflin, American Folklore Society, 1904.**

> The richness of Pawnee religion and cosmology is woven through this major collection of narratives infused with bright imagery and the voices of storytellers.

Eastman, Charles A. *Smoky Day's Wigwam Evenings: Indian Stories Retold.* **Boston: Little, Brown, 1910.**

The simple narrative style draws the reader deeply into the drama and humor of these Sioux tales of strange beasts, heroes, and stories of Unktomee, the spider, who with mischievous cunning could change into a man or an animal.

Fisher, Anne. *Stories California Indians Told.* **Berkeley, CA: Parnassus Press, 1957.**

Wonderful stories from the Pomo, Yokuts, Karok, Mono, Gabrielino, Miwok, and Achomawi tribes recount events in the early days of the world, such as how Old-Man-Above made Mt. Shasta, and how the Great Spirit made California on the backs of the Turtle Brothers. Ingenuity and daring are central themes throughout.

Gifford, Edward W., and Block, Gwendoline H. *California Indian Nights Entertainments: Stories of the Creation of the World, of Man, of Fire, of the Sun, of Thunder, Etc.* **Glendale, CA: Arthur H. Clark Co., 1930.**

The great diversity of California tribes and their stories is reflected here, especially in "Coyote and the Land of the Dead" and more than eighty myths and tales from California's principal regions.

Gillham, Charles E. *Beyond the Clapping Mountains: Eskimo Stories from Alaska.* **New York: Macmillan, 1943.**

Fine black-and-white line drawings by Chanimun, a young Eskimo girl, enliven these thirteen stories about birds and animals that once lived and acted as real people.

———. *Medicine Men of Hooper Bay: More Tales from the Clapping Mountains of Alaska.* **New York: Macmillan, 1955.**

Further tales of medicine men (shamans) with powerful magic and orphan children who could see elves, fairies, and dwarfs invisible to others.

Goodwin, Grenville. *Myths and Tales of the White Mountain Apache.* **New York: American Folklore Society, 1939.**

Adventures of Coyote and Big Owl, and stories of the Gaan, who are supernatural mountain spirits.

Grinnell, George Bird. *Blackfoot Lodge Tales: The Story of a Prairie People.* **Lincoln: University of Nebraska Press, Bison Books, 1962.**

Explores four major categories of Blackfoot tales: origin of rituals and magical transformations; warriors' adventures; incidents of camp life; and entertaining accounts of "Old Man."

————. *By Cheyenne Campfires.* **New Haven: Yale University Press, 1962.**

Valuable historical narratives, myths, and folktales gathered over the author's forty years of work among the dynamic Plains Indian cultures.

————. *Pawnee Hero Stories and Folk-Tales: With Notes on the Origin, Customs, and Character of the Pawnee People.* **Lincoln: University of Nebraska Press, 1961.**

Further classics and "miraculous doings of the olden times" are spun out of literal translations.

————. *The Punishment of the Stingy, and other Indian Stories.* **New York: Harper Publishing, 1901.**

Legendary stories from aged historians among the Pawnee, Blackfeet, and Northwest Coast People—filled with magic powers, kindness, courage, and the rich flavors of earlier life.

Hooke, Hilda M. *Thunder in the Mountains: Legends of Canada.* **Toronto: Oxford University Press, 1947.**

Anthology of fourteen folktales representing sections of traditional life in Canada and Labrador.

Johnston, Basil H. *Tales the Elders Told: Ojibway Legends.* **Toronto: Royal Ontario Museum, 1981.**

These jewel-like stories share knowledge and understanding from one generation to another.

Keithalan, Edward L. *Alaskan Igloo Tales.* **Seattle: R. D. Seal, 1958.**

Fabulous tales of witchcraft, sorcery, and "robber dwarfs" are embellished with pencil drawings by George A. Ahgupuk, an Eskimo schoolboy.

Kilpatrick, Jack F., and Kilpatrick, Anna G., eds. *Friends of Thunder: Folktales of the Oklahoma Cherokees.* **Dallas: Southern Methodist University Press, 1964.**

Captures the art of storytelling among the Oklahoma Cherokee, along with fragmentary versions of old recollections.

Kimball, Teffe, and Leekley, Thomas B. *The World of Manabozho: Tales of the Chippewa Indians.* **New York: Vanguard Press, 1965.**

Chippewa and Ottawa stories, with parallels in Blackfeet and Cree folklore, make use of the hero-cycle storytelling pattern.

Kroeber, Theodora. *The Inland Whale.* **Bloomington: Indiana University Press, 1959.**

Absorbing stories spun from the folklore and mythology of the California Indians illustrate the impressive literature and values of their rich culture.

Linderman, Frank B. *Indian Why Stories: Sparks from War Eagle's Lodge-Fire.* **New York: Scribner, 1915.**

Classic stories from the Blackfeet, Chippewa, and Cree in traditional storytelling style: spirited, humorous, and enthusiastic.

Lowie, Robert H. *Myths and Traditions of the Crow Indians.* **Anthropological Papers, Vol. 25. New York: American Museum of Natural History, 1918.**

The historical development of Crow Indian mythology, human heroes, and supernatural heroic beings are the subject of this distinctive work.

Marriott, Alice L. *Winter-Telling Stories.* **New York: W. Sloane Associates, 1947.**

Colorful Kiowa trickster-transformer Saynday spins eleven tales of "good" and "bad" with lots of room in between for trouble and great humor. Wonderful Kiowa color illustrations.

———. *Saynday's People: The Kiowa Indians and the Stories They Told.* **Lincoln: University of Nebraska Press, 1963.**

The "timelessness and universality of the trickster-transformer Saynday" are explored again here.

Martin, Frances G. *Nine Tales of Raven.* **New York: Harper Publishing, 1951.**

Myths of the Tsimshian, Bellabella, Kwakiutl, and Tlingit Indians illustrate the two sides of Raven's character in the magical worlds of Northwest Coast culture, where Raven is a respected creation figure.

Mooney, James. *Myths of the Cherokee.* **Asheville, NC: Historical Images, 1992.**

An extensive collection of myths and traditions gathered from the Cherokee on the Qualla Reservation in North

Carolina from 1887 to 1890, with valuable background and historical sketches.

Mourning Dove. *Coyote Stories*. **Caldwell, ID: Caxton Printers, 1933.**

Sensitive background and explanations supplement the telling of these selected tales, wherein Spirit Chief gives Coyote the responsibility for making the world ready for humans and ridding it of "People-Devouring Monsters." The colorful narrative style of the storyteller shines through.

Parker, Arthur C. *Skunny Wundy: Seneca Indian Tales*. **New York: Albert Whitman & Co., 1970.**

Classic stories originally published in 1926, and enduring in the Iroquois tradition of using animal tales to teach life's lessons.

Radin, Paul. *The Culture of the Winnebago: As Described by Themselves*. **Baltimore: Waverly Press, 1949.**

Complete story cycles demonstrate the fine narrative style and authentic literature of a Great Lakes culture.

Rasmussen, Knud, ed. and trans. *The Eagle's Gift: Alaska Eskimo Tales*. **Garden City, NY: Doubleday, 1932.**

These classic tales and traditions were collected by Knud Rasmussen, who led the Fifth Thule Expedition (1921–24) across Arctic America. Raven and Wander-Hawk stories are shared in a wonderful storytelling cycle, generous with supernatural elements.

Running, Corinne. *When Coyote Walked the Earth: Indian Tales of the Pacific Northwest*. **New York: Henry Holt, 1949.**

Beautifully illustrated, these fourteen Coyote tales from the time when only animals lived on earth echo rich

Indian oral traditions, and we learn that Coyote is always present.

Swanton, John R. *Tlingit Myths and Texts*. Washington, DC: Government Printing Office, Smithsonian Institution, 1909.

Issued as House Document 1528, U.S. 60th Congress, 2nd session. Literal translations of myths and texts collected by a famous ethnographer at Sitka and Wrangell, Alaska, in 1904.

Zuni People of Zuni Pueblo. *The Zunis: Self-Portrayals*. Translated by Alvina Quam. Albuquerque: University of New Mexico Press, 1972.

Forty-six stories from the great Zuni oral literature, detailing their creation story, rituals of masked dances, farming and hunting practices, and much more. Robert E. Lewis, Zuni governor, writes in his introduction, "We are proud to present this, the first volume of stories told by the oldest members of my Zuni people."

FILMS AND VIDEOS

The Native American Public Broadcasting Consortium (NAPBC) provides a growing number of valuable resources, including an impressive film and video catalog, from which you may purchase or rent some of the following selections.

NAPBC
1800 North 33rd Street
P.O. Box 83111
Lincoln, NE 68501-3111
402-472-3522

***Ancient Spirit, Living Word: The Oral Tradition*. KBDI-TV, 1983.**

Passed by word of mouth from generation to generation, the oral tradition is both a link to the past and a key to the future.

Art of Being Indian: Filmed Aspects of the Culture of the Sioux. **South Dakota ETV, 1976.**

An overview of the Sioux from their early days to their present status.

Broken Rainbow, **1985. Directed and produced by Maria Floria and Victoria Mudd.**

A powerful movie about the Navajo relocation, which draws parallels to earlier cruelty in Navajo history. It won an Oscar for best documentary film in 1985.

Children of the Long-Beaked Bird. **Bullfrog Films, 1976.**

Moving portrait of Dominic Old Elk, a twelve-year-old Crow boy who is proud of his heritage.

Dancing to Give Thanks. **Nebraska Educational TV, 1980.**

The traditions and family customs of the Omaha tribe are celebrated at their 184th annual He-De-Wa-Chi, or Festival of Joy.

Dineh: The People. **Tiresias Film Production, 1976.**

Award-winning documentary focusing on the Navajo relocation period, which began in the mid-1970s with the passage of the Navajo-Hopi Land Settlement Act (1974). The act forced the removal of thousands of Navajo families whose homesteads encroached upon Hopi lands.

Distant Voices . . . Thunder Words. **Nebraska Educational TV, 1990.**

This program explores the influence of oral traditions on contemporary Native American storytellers and writers.

Folklore of the Muscogee (Creek) People. **Gary Robinson/Creek National Communications and KOED-TV, 1983.**

Traditional Creek legends, myths, and fables are described and explored.

Forest Spirits—A Series. **NEWIST, 1975–76.**

Filmed on location in Wisconsin, with footage of the Oneida Nation and the Menominee people, this series explores a broad range of cultural traditions.

Forgotten Frontier. **KAET-TV, 1976.**

An exploration of Spanish mission settlements of southern Arizona where Jesuit and Franciscan priests "created a cultural climate for conversion rather than baptizing by force."

Four Corners of Earth. **Bureau of Florida Folklife and WFSU-TV, 1985.**

Seminole women's traditional values and roles within their distinctive culture are explored through foods, medical practices, clan systems, legends, traditional clothing, crafts, and education.

Gannagaro. **WXXI-TV, 1986.**

An archaeological look at a historic seventeenth-century Seneca village destroyed by the French in July 1687.

Grandfather Sky. **Chariot Productions, KAET-TV, and NAPBC, 1983.**

Contemporary story of Charlie Lone Wolf, a troubled urban Lakota/Navajo youth, whose emerging knowledge of his heritage and sense of identity is resonant for today's youth.

I Am Different from My Brother: Dakota Name-Giving. **NAPBC, 1981.**

Depicts a traditional name-giving ceremony for three young Flandreau Dakota Sioux Indian children, as they learn more about honor, self-worth, and their rich cultural traditions.

Images of Indians—A Series. **KCTS/9 Seattle, 1981.**

Narrated by Will Sampson, the legendary Creek actor. Five thirty-minute features explore the dubious "cowboy and Indian" film industry since 1913. Installments include the Great Movie Massacre; Heathen Injuns and the Hollywood Gospel; How Hollywood Wins the West; The Movie Reel Indians; and Warpaint & Wigs.

In the White Man's Image. **NAPBC and Nebraska Educational TV, 1991.**

Examination of the 1875 educational experiment that established the Carlisle Indian School and the consequences of the experiment for a generation of Indians.

More than Bows and Arrows. **13th Regional Corp./ Camera One, 1992.**

An outstanding broad perspective and overview of Native American history, narrated by noted Kiowa scholar and writer N. Scott Momaday.

Nations Within a Nation. **Produced by Oklahoma State University Department of Sociology, 1986.**

Examines issues of sovereignty of Native American nations, and the historical, legal, and social aspects of this issue.

New Pequot: A Tribal Portrait. **Connecticut Public Television, 1983.**

Valuable documentary exploring the history and future of Connecticut's Mashantucket Pequot Indians, who have come back from the brink of extermination to become one of the brightest American Indian success stories.

Nez Perce—Portrait of a People. **Phil Lucas, 1983.**

A fascinating, accurate story of the incredible history of the Nez Perce.

On the Path to Self-Reliance. **Peter J. Barton Productions, 1982.**

Documentary overview of the Seminole tribe of Florida, narrated by Chair James Billie, showing how the tribe is realizing its goal of self-sufficiency and maintaining its cultural heritage and identity.

People of the First Light—A Series. **WGBY-TV, 1979.**

Cultural identity, traditions, and tribal history of the Native Americans of southern New England are explored, highlighting the states of Massachusetts, Rhode Island, and Connecticut.

Pueblo Peoples: "First Encounter." **KNME-TV, 1991.**

Weaves historic accounts of the first Spanish invaders in 1539–40 with an exploration of cultural and spiritual dimensions.

Real People—A Series. **KSPS-TV, 1976.**

The first TV series made by and about American Indians, it explores broad aspects of cultural traditions from "A Season of Grandmothers" to "Circles of Songs" and much more.

Chapter 6
Genealogical Records and Research

The key to knowledge is knowing where to find the information you need. Researching family history is like detective work, and your "clues" are contained in family documents such as marriage, birth, and death certificates. Focus on your objectives, and patiently gather your essential facts. Taking oral histories and documenting family folklore are valuable and rewarding tasks, yet for tribal documentation and genealogical verification you need proof. Your grandmother may say that she was born at home on the farm and delivered by the family doctor or a midwife on March 3, 1923, in Asbury, Tennessee. Yet you must have the birth certificate for genealogical proof. Cross-reference your important documents so that you can find them easily and settle any disputes about dates, places, and circumstances.

Start with yourself. Write down your full name, birth date and place, and where you've lived. Write down these same details for your brothers and sisters. Get their help and participation with this, if you can. Gather this same information from your parents, along with the date and place of their marriage. See if you can locate family copies of birth and marriage certificates and social security numbers. Get this same information from each of your grandparents and from their parents, if possible, and write down all the vital details you can. Move back through time, step by step, and create easy forms to organize this information, like the ones provided in this book. Work your way back through time in an orderly way.

Don't jump around chronologically, especially in the beginning. It may be tempting to start with your great-great-grandfather, who fought in the War of 1812, if you find his life especially fascinating. But you must first move backward from yourself, and don't skip generations. Don't get frustrated if you can't find every date and detail. Make blank spaces where the needed data should go, and move on to another branch of the family tree, or research another family line. Just reaching for your roots can be fascinating. See if you can go back more than three generations.

Every little bit counts. You do not have to complete the project immediately. For some of us, the journey lasts a lifetime. Gaining a sense of yourself and your place within your family, culture, traditions, and history is a fine goal.

Where to Write for Vital Records: Births, Deaths, Marriages, and Divorces is an inexpensive booklet published by the U.S. Department of Health and Human Services. It lists the name and address of each state's vital records agency, the current cost of ordering a record, and the dates for which these records are available. Vital records are often necessary for obtaining tribal enrollment or proving specific family descents. Professional genealogists consider nothing a fact unless they have a document to verify it.

Statewide registration of vital records started in the early 1900s, and most states have vital records from about 1910 to the present. If you know the state and town in which a person was born or died, you can write for specific birth and death records. There may be a small fee for this service. A birth certificate should contain the name of a person's father and the maiden name of the mother along with the date and place of birth.

A death certificate can be an important starting point to learn where, how, and when that relative died, along with (perhaps) the date and place of birth. This might enable you to write for the birth certificate, which should have additional verifying data on it. You may also request a funeral record, cemetery record, obituary, and social security number. The fees are usually five to seven dollars per document.

When you receive these valuable documents, be sure to file them, or copies of them, in a safe, well-organized fashion. Set up your own system of family notebooks and files to suit your space and needs. Make a file for each person. Be prepared for it to grow—as it surely will—through the years as you build up information in your quest for family history, tribal membership, or information regarding your ancestors' movements and lives.

Library Resources

Investigate all that you can easily gain from your family, and then head to your local library. Ask the librarians for help, and search through the reference books on family associations and newsletters, historical and genealogical societies, libraries and town halls, county seats, and cemetery associations.

Libraries can be some of your best tools for genealogical research. Some libraries have microfilm and microfiche equipment to enable you to search through census records and other documents, for example. Larger libraries may have specific genealogy or local history departments. Librarians will be happy to help you find the materials you need. What the library does not have you may be able to borrow from another library through interlibrary loan.

The Family History Library in Salt Lake City, Utah, is operated by the Church of Jesus Christ of Latter-day Saints (LDS). This library is open to the public and contains voluminous resources for genealogical research. You may not be able to travel to Salt Lake City, but there are over 1,000 branches of the Family History Library, called Family History Centers, with computer facilities available for surveying genealogical resources.

Check your local phone book under "Church of Jesus Christ of Latter-day Saints." Or, write to the main branch for a listing of local centers.

The holdings of the LDS Library include published family histories, county records, vital records, atlases, and passenger lists. The LDS also provides a Family Registry service, where people looking for information on a certain family line can fill out a form and make their search known to others who might have information. This form is available at Family History Centers.

Census Records

Beginning in 1790, the U.S. Constitution stipulated that a nationwide census of the population be taken every ten years. The first five censuses listed the names of the heads of households living in every state from 1790 through 1840. These are treasured resources for genealogists needing particulars of when and where people lived.

The names of every member of a household were first listed in 1850, making the federal census schedules tremendously valuable for locating American individuals and families. Unfortunately, a fire at the National Archives destroyed most census records through 1880.

The census records the names of household members, their addresses, ages, and some personal information. To search for information about your family, you must choose a census year and check the census of the town where you believe a relative lived in that year. Information gathered from the census should still be checked against vital records.

Old census name lists survive in the National Archives in Washington, DC. The Congress passed a law protecting the privacy of every person named in a federal census for a period of seventy-two years, so 1920 is the most recent census year for which records are available. In addition to the National Archives, these population schedules are also available on microfilm at some libraries and archives. See the **Resources** at the end of this chapter for more information on searching census records.

Soundex Index

Beginning with the 1920 census, a Soundex index was made for every head of household in all states and territories. A Soundex index is a unifying asset for streamlining genealogical research. The method removes from a name extra letters that sound alike, all vowels, and double letters, and then codes the hard sounds of the remaining letters. This enables you to find a person in the census whose surname can be spelled a variety of ways. Originally prepared by the Works Progress Administration in the 1930s, the Soundex index

Your genealogical research may lead you to discover your ancestors' traditional Indian names, which are often evocative of nature or personality traits. The Indian name of Chief Joseph of the Nez Perce was Hinmaton Yalatket, which means "Thunder coming from the water up over the land." This photo shows Chief Joseph in 1900.

has been almost completed for each federal census back to 1790. Talk to your local librarian or a librarian at a Family History Center about using the Soundex.

Native American Names

Census takers often wrote Native American names and surnames phonetically, as best they could. Some surnames change drastically from one document to another over time. Most tribal peoples never had two names as we do today. A Native American baby was often given a "birth name" by an important family elder. Later, as a young boy or girl approached puberty, he or she might prepare for this next major phase of life by participating in a formal naming ceremony. A new name often remained with the individual throughout his or her life. In some tribes, this name was so sacred that it was not spoken outside of the family, clan, or tribal group. Another name was used instead.

Many Native Americans received additional names based upon life deeds, visions and vision quests, feats of bravery, or forces of nature. Some received Christian names when they embraced a particular faith or participated in the census.

For purposes of clarity, make a note of all names an individual was known by. Determine which name (or names) were used in official documents. Do not discard nonofficial names, however; these can be fascinating details to add to a written family history or illustrated family tree.

Wills and Cemeteries

Wills, where they exist, are filled with important and interesting details about families. I still recall our enthusiasm when my cousin Gail found Great-Granddaddy Morris's forty-page handwritten will and got it copied in an Alabama courthouse. Some wills are almost books in themselves. Reading and deciphering old wills is a little like visiting with one's ancestors at a turning point in family history. Ask if family members have copies of wills; if not, check with the town or county courthouse in the place where your ancestor died.

Cemeteries, family plots, and cemetery records are additional sources of family data. Sometimes the cemetery where the person is buried is mentioned in the death certificate. It is usually worthwhile to check whether there is a record in the cemetery office.

A gravestone inscription may reveal details about your family. Your visit to the cemetery can be an opportunity to pay respect to your ancestors in addition to gathering information about them. My friend Wendell Deer with Horns, Lakota, Two Kettles Band, from Cheyenne River Sioux Reservation in Eagle Butte, South Dakota, recalls going to the family cemetery plot each Sunday, as a child, with his mother during the 1950s. They would take flowers and little bits of food, and a small jar of hot coffee or soup, and make a "spirit plate" for the spirits of all their dead relatives. These offerings were accompanied with prayers, and sometimes songs, to reassure loved ones that they were remembered. Similar practices for remembering the deceased are followed in many Native American cultures.

The Association for Gravestone Studies, 46 Plymouth Road, Needham, MA 02192, publishes a brochure describing books and leaflets about cemeteries and gravestones. You may become inspired to do "tombstone anthropology," studying the type of stone used, the design, and the inscriptions.

Many early "family plots" and private unmarked graves exist in countless areas where Native Americans once lived. Some say the spirits still walk the land, and you can feel an ancient presence in numerous locales that were once favorite meeting places, trading and dance grounds, ceremonial and residential places. Patient research may yield information about your own ancestors' resting places.

Historical and Family Associations

More than 1,500 genealogy clubs nationwide are gathering and sharing resources, and many have volunteer researchers who may be able to help you in your search. Some may expect a small donation to their society for this help. Inquire first to see if they have any Native American materials and documents that might be useful to you. Many do not, or do not know if they do.

Local, state, and regional historical societies are valuable sources of family histories. Many historical societies have local volunteers who are themselves valuable resources. Most of them love to share their information, especially with young people. They often know where the surrounding cemeteries and cemetery records are located. It is best to write ahead to a historical society you wish to visit and specify the kind of information you need, so that they can be prepared. It can take a while for your written request to get to the right person in these volunteer organizations. Don't be offended if you do not get an immediate answer.

Many historical societies throughout New England have impressive collections of prehistoric projectile points, adzes (cutting tools), mortars and pestles, calendar stones, and other fascinating stone tools. These often serve to illuminate more than 10,000 years of human habitation in these regions. Yet they might not have many written resources on Native American history. Native American artifacts can still be found, in varying degrees, all over the continent. Walking through an ordinary corn field in Connecticut, you might come across a quartz spear point, a flint knife, or a basalt sinew stone.

Many historical societies, national historic sites, and national parks are rich resources for Native American culture. Investigate these national treasures, and take notes, sketching particular sites and objects that interest you. Remember to write down all the information you can about each site for future reference. Visiting these facilities will deepen your understanding of your family's history.

If you walk around New York City, Chicago, Los Angeles, and other major cities, you are walking on ancient Indian land. You can almost feel the presence of prehistoric peoples who once lived, camped, hunted, and traded there. The fossilized bones of mastodons were found by workers excavating and enlarging the subway system under the streets of

Documents are available describing the allotment of land to the Five Civilized Tribes. Among these five are the Seminoles, representatives of which are seen here returning from a visit to a neighboring tribe in 1919.

Manhattan. Who were the ancient people who once hunted here? They might be your ancestors.

Records in the National Archives

The original records of the headquarters of the Bureau of Indian Affairs are in the National Archives in Washington, DC, along with many records relating to Indians who maintained their tribal affiliations. Most of the records, arranged by tribe, cover the years 1830 to 1940. They include:

- Lists of Indians (primarily Cherokee, Creek, Chickasaw, and Choctaw) who moved west during the 1830–1846 removal period. Entries on these lists usually contain the names of family heads; number, age, and sex of family members; description of property owned before removal; and dates of leaving the East and arriving in the West.

- Annuity payrolls, 1841–1949, record the name, age, and sex of the heads of families that received an annual government payment.
- Annual census rolls, 1885–1940 (available on microfilm); the Indian and English names are usually shown for each person in a family, along with age, sex, and relationship to the head of the family.
- Applications for enrollment and allotment of land to individual tribal members of the Five Civilized Tribes. The original applications for enrollment of Cherokees, Creeks, Chickasaws, Choctaws, and Seminoles by the Dawes Commission, 1898–1907, are available on microfilm.
- Eastern Cherokee claim files, 1902–1910, with name, residence, date and place of birth, name and age of spouse, names of father, mother, and children, and other genealogical information about claimants. The National Archives staff will search these files if you can supply the full name, both Indian and English, of the applicant. The identifying information should be sent to the General Reference Branch (NNRG), National Archives, Washington, DC (preferably on NATF form 83, Order for Copies of Eastern Cherokee Applications). More than 692 rolls of microfilm on all federally recognized tribes throughout the United States, and the Indian Census Rolls for 1885 through 1940, are on file at the National Archives Records of Washington, DC, Bureau of Indian Affairs, Record Group 75 M-595.
- Some of the tribes in the United States and Canada have established their own tribal libraries and family records depositories, drawn from BIA records, missionary and Indian boarding school records, and the records of other research libraries, especially the LDS Libraries of the Church of Jesus Christ of Latter-day Saints (Mormons), based in Utah.
- Reference Librarian Eugene Mark Felsman, a Pend

From your search, you can discover your ancestors' places in history. Perhaps you will find from military records that some of your relatives served in the armed forces, like the Native American soldiers depicted here, who were in training for combat in World War II.

d'Oreille/Piegan Blackfeet Indian, has developed extensive resources during his twelve years at the D'Arcy McNickle Library at Salish Kootenai College in Pablo, Montana, where he established a Family History Center for the Salish, Kootenai, and Pend d'Oreille tribes. He wrote the article "Researching Native Roots" in the fall 1995 issue of *TRIBAL COL-LEGE: Journal of American Indian Higher Education* (Vol. VII(2): Mancos, Colorado). In it he details his quest for genealogical data and his time spent poring through old newspapers and investigating veteran records in the Indian War Papers in Washington, DC.

- Military records are available on individuals who served in the Army, Navy, or Marines. Native Americans have served the United States with distinction in many battles. Perhaps one of your ancestors was one of the "Code Talkers" who used Indian languages to transmit messages that would not be understood by the enemy. Choctaw, Comanche, and Navajo soldiers performed this vital function in World War II. Requests for information on individuals who served since 1900 should be addressed to: Military Personnel Records, 9700 Page Boulevard, St. Louis, MO 63132. You might also try the American Indian Veterans Association, P.O. Box 543, Isleta, MN 87022; 505-869-9284.

Computers and Genealogy

Computers are among the most useful tools available to genealogists. While a computer cannot do your research for you, there are many software packages available to help you organize your findings.

The Family History Library of the Church of Jesus Christ of Latter-day Saints has developed a software package called Personal Ancestral File (PAF). The Family Records program of PAF allows you to enter birth, death, and marriage information on your ancestors, and organizes it in chart form. PAF, and other genealogy software packages, allow you to print out charts, family group sheets, family trees, and other important visual and organizational tools.

The Internet is another tool used by many genealogists to gather information and share results with others. Genealogy discussion groups and bulletin boards allow users to communicate with other genealogists on a huge variety of general and specific topics. You may decide to communicate your results with relatives or conduct interviews via e-mail (electronic mail).

The home pages listed in the **Resources** section at the end of this chapter are of particular importance to genealogists. You might also want to see what pops up when you do a general Internet search using terms such as "Native American Genealogy," "American Indian Genealogy," or the name of your specific tribe. Many tribes now have their own home pages. The offerings on the Internet are constantly changing, so don't be discouraged if a home page that existed last week doesn't seem to be found anywhere this week. For every home page or website that seems to be "lost," there is probably another equally exciting one that has just appeared.

Resources

USING OUTSIDE SOURCES

Bentley, Elizabeth P. *County Courthouse Book.* **Baltimore: Genealogical Publishing Co., 1994.**

> Detailed information on the 3,351 county courthouses in the United States, with addresses, phone numbers, and record holdings.

———. *Directory of Family Associations.* **Baltimore: Genealogical Publishing Co., 1993.**

> Listings of the 6,000 family associations in the United States, with addresses and phone numbers.

National Archives and Records Administration. *Genealogical Records in the National Archives.* **Washington, DC: General Services Administration.**

> A general information leaflet detailing the resources at this huge holding center, and how to locate what you need.

———. *Genealogical Sources Outside the National Archives.* **Washington, DC: General Services Administration.**

> A leaflet detailing many additional records and resources, and where to find them.

NAMES

Smith, Elsdon C. *American Surnames.* **Baltimore: Genealogical Publishing Co., 1994.**

> For exploring and explaining the roots and meanings of surnames, especially Indian names, this book is a valuable reference guide.

CENSUS RECORDS

Alterman, Hyman. *Counting People: The Census in History*. **New York: Harcourt Brace, 1969.**

Valuable early reference, especially the American Indian data on pages 291–304.

Lainhart, Ann S. *State Census Records*. **Baltimore: Genealogical Publishing Co., 1992.**

An authoritative guide to state censuses, showing what is available in county, district, and state records from year to year.

Silfer, David. *The Eastern Cherokees: A Census of the Cherokee Nation in North Carolina, Tennessee, Alabama, and Georgia in 1851*. **New Orleans: Polyanthos, 1977.**

Remarkable data in 150 pages, providing valuable references for Cherokee historians.

Thorndale, William, and Dollarhide, William. *Map Guide to the U.S. Federal Censuses, 1790–1920*. **Baltimore: Genealogical Publishing Co., 1991.**

Shows all U.S. county boundaries from 1790 to 1920 to assist you in locating the census that corresponds to your ancestor's county of residence.

GRAVES AND CEMETERIES

Jacobs, G. Walker. *Stranger Stop and Cast an Eye: A Guide to Gravestones and Gravestone Rubbing*. **Brattleboro, VT: S. Greene Press, 1973.**

Gravestone rubbing can be a way to make a paper record of a relative's gravestone. You can frame the rubbing or make it an illustration in your family history. Rubbings also allow you to record your visit to a family cemetery.

NATIONAL ARCHIVES

Hill, Edward E., ed. *Guide to Records in the National Archives Relating to American Indians*. Washington, DC: National Archives Publications Sales Branch, 1981.

> Comprehensive review and description of National Archives holdings on Native Americans; more than 465 pages of fascinating data and photos.

National Archives and Records Administration
Eighth Street and Pennsylvania Avenue NW
Washington, DC 20408
202-501-5400

> Available records include census schedules, land records, passenger lists, passport applications, personnel records, pension and bounty land claims, military records, and specific records on Native Americans.

NATIONAL ARCHIVES REGIONAL ARCHIVES

Alaska
National Archives
Alaska Office
Federal Office Building
654 West Third Avenue
Anchorage, AK 99501
907-271-2441

Central Plains States
National Archives
Central Plains Region
2312 East Bannister Road
Kansas City, MO 64131
816-926-6272

> Records on Iowa, Kansas, Missouri, Nebraska.

Great Lakes States
National Archives
Great Lakes Region
7358 South Pulaski Road
Chicago, IL 60629
312-581-7816

Records on Illinois, Indiana, Michigan, Minnesota, Ohio, Wisconsin.

Mid-Atlantic States
National Archives
Mid-Atlantic Region
9th and Market Streets
Philadelphia, PA 19107
215-597-3000

Records on Delaware, Maryland, Pennsylvania, Virginia, West Virginia.

New England States
National Archives
New England Region
380 Trapelo Road
Waltham, MA 02154
617-647-8100

Records on Connecticut, Maine, Massachusetts, New Hampshire, Rhode Island, Vermont.

Northeastern States
National Archives
Northeast Region
201 Varick Street
New York, NY 10014
212-337-1300

Records on New Jersey, New York, Puerto Rico, Virgin Islands.

Pacific Northwest
National Archives

Pacific Northwest Region
6125 Sand Point Way, NE
Seattle, WA 98115
206-526-6507

Records on Idaho, Oregon, Washington.

Pacific Sierra
National Archives
Pacific Sierra Region
1000 Commodore Drive
San Bruno, CA 94066
415-876-9009

Records on Hawaii, Nevada, northern California.

Pacific Southwest
National Archives
Pacific Southwest Region
24000 Avila Road
Laguna Niguel, CA 92656
714-643-4241

Records on Arizona, southern California, Nevada's Clark County.

Rocky Mountain States
National Archives
Rocky Mountain Region
Building 48, Denver Federal Center
P.O. Box 25307
Denver, CO 80225
303-236-0817

Records on Colorado, Montana, North Dakota, South Dakota, Utah, Wyoming.

Southeastern States
National Archives

Southeast Region
1557 St. Joseph Avenue
East Point, GA 30344
404-763-7477

> Records on Alabama, Georgia, Florida, Kentucky, Mississippi, North Carolina, South Carolina, Tennessee.

Southwestern States
National Archives
Southwest Region
501 West Felix Street
Ft. Worth, TX 76115
817-334-5525

> Records on Arkansas, Louisiana, New Mexico, Oklahoma, Texas.

HISTORICAL SOCIETIES, GENEALOGICAL SOCIETIES, AND LIBRARIES

Alabama
Mobile Public Library
Local History and Genealogy Division
701 Government Street
Mobile, AL 36602
205-434-7093

Poarch Creek Indian Heritage Center Library
P.O. Box 633
Wetumpka, AL 36092
205-567-7800

Alaska
Anchorage Museum of History and Art Library
121 West Seventh Avenue
Anchorage, AK 99501
907-343-4326

Elmer E. Rasmuson Library
University of Alaska
Fairbanks, AK 99701

Sheldon Museum and Cultural Center Library
P.O. Box 269
Haines, AK 99827

Sitka National Historical Park Library
106 Metlakatla
P.O. Box 738
Sitka, AK 99835
907-747-6281

Arizona
Arizona Library
Archives and Public Records
Genealogy Library
1700 West Washington, State Capitol
Phoenix, AZ 85007
602-542-3942

Arkansas
Arkansas State University Museum Library and
   Archives
P.O. Box 490
State University
Jonesboro, AR 72467
501-972-2074

California
American Indian Studies Center Library
3220 Campbell Hall
University of California, Los Angeles
Los Angeles, CA 90024
310-825-7315

Los Angeles Public Library
History and Genealogy Department
433 South Spring Street

Los Angeles, CA 90071
213-612-3314

Native American Studies Library
University of California
343 Dwinelle Hall
Berkeley, CA 94720

Southern California Genealogical Society Library
122 South San Fernando Boulevard
P.O. Box 4377
Burbank, CA 91503
818-843-7247

Colorado
National Indian Law Library
Native American Rights Fund
1522 Broadway
Boulder, CO 80302-6296
303-447-8760

Connecticut
Institute for American Indian Studies Research and
    Education Library
Curtis Road
Washington, CT 06793
203-868-0518

Mashantucket Pequot Tribal Museum Library and
    Research System
Indiantown Road
Ledyard, CT 06339
203-536-7200

Pequot Library
720 Pequot Avenue
Southport, CT 06490
203-259-0346

Delaware
Nanticoke Indian Museum Library

Route 4, Box 107A
Millsboro, DE 19966

District of Columbia
Library of Congress
Local History and Genealogy Reading Room
10 First Street SE
Washington, DC 20540
202-287-5537

National Indian Education Association Library
1819 H Street NW
Washington, DC 20006

Natural Resources Library
U.S. Department of the Interior
1849 C Street NW
Washington, DC 20240
202-208-5815

U.S. Department of the Interior Library
18th and C Streets NW
Washington, DC 20240
202-343-5810

U.S. Department of Justice Environment Library
10th Street and Pennsylvania Avenue NW
Washington, DC 20530
202-514-2768

Florida
Florida Historical Society Library
University of South Florida
Tampa, FL 33620

Seminole Tribe Library
6073 Stirling Road
Hollywood, FL 33024
305-964-4860

Temple Mound Museum Library
P.O. Box 4009

139 Miraclestrip Parkway SE
Fort Walton Beach, FL 32548
904-243-6521

Georgia
New Echota Historic Site Library
1211 Chatsworth Highway
Calhoun, GA 30701
404-629-8151

Ocmulgee National Monument Library
1207 Emery Highway
Macon, GA 31201
912-742-0447

Idaho
Idaho State Historical Society Library
610 North Julia Drive
Boise, ID 83702
208-334-3356

Nez Perce National Historical Park Library
P.O. Box 93
Spalding, ID 83551
208-843-2261

Illinois
Cahokia Mounds State Historic Site Library
7850 Collinsville Road
East St. Louis, IL 62201
618-344-5268

Illinois State Historical Library
Old State Capitol
Springfield, IL 62701

Newberry Library
D'Arcy McNickle Center for the History of the American Indian
60 West Walton Street
Chicago, IL 60610
312-943-9090

Indiana
Indiana University Museum Library
Student Building 107
Bloomington, IN 47401

Museum of Indian Heritage
Reference Library
500 West Washington Street
Indianapolis, IN 46204
317-293-4488

Potawatomi Museum Library
P.O. Box 486
North Wayne and City Limits
Fremont, IN 46737

Iowa
Effigy Mounds National Monument Library
RR 1, Box 25A
Harpers Ferry, IA 52146
319-873-3491

Iowa State Historical Museum Library
East 12th Street and Grande Avenue
Des Moines, IA 50319
515-281-5111

State Historical Society of Iowa Library
402 Iowa Avenue
Iowa City, IA 52240-1806
319-335-3916

Kansas
Kansas State Historical Society Library
120 West 10th Street
Topeka, KS 66612-1291
913-296-4776

Mid-America All Indian Center Library
650 North Seneca Street
Wichita, KS 67203

Pawnee Indian Village Museum Library
Rt. 1, Box 475
Republic, KS 66964
913-361-2255

Kentucky
Kentucky Historical Society Library
300 Broadway
Frankfort, KY 40602
502-564-3016

Louisiana
Grindstone Bluff Museum Library
501 Jenkins Road
P.O. Box 7965
Shreveport, LA 71107

Louisiana State Archives
P.O. Box 94125, Capitol Station
Baton Rouge, LA 70804
504-922-1207

Maine
Maine Tribal Unity Museum Library
Quaker Hill Road
Unity, ME 04988
207-948-3131

Robert Abbe Museum of Stone Age Antiquity Library
P.O. Box 286
Bar Harbor, ME 04609
207-288-3519

Massachusetts
Boston Indian Council Library
105 South Huntington Street
Jamaica Plain, MA 02130
617-232-0343

New England Historic Genealogical Society Library
101 Newbury Street

Boston, MA 02116
617-536-5740

Plimoth Plantation Library
P.O. Box 1620
Plymouth, MA 02362
508-746-1622

Michigan
Cranbrook Institute of Science
500 Lone Pine Road, Box 801
Bloomfield Hills, MI 48303
313-645-3260

Detroit Public Library
Burton Historical Collection
5201 Woodward Avenue
Detroit, MI 48202
313-833-1480

Genesee Indian Center Library
124 West First Street
Flint, MI 48502-1311

University of Michigan—William L. Clements Library
South University Street
Ann Arbor, MI 48104

Minnesota
Becker County Historical Society Library
915 Lake Avenue
Detroit Lakes, MN 56501

Minnesota Historical Society
1500 Mississippi Street
St. Paul, MN 55101
612-296-6980

Mississippi
Grand Village of the Natchez Indians Library
400 Jefferson Davis Boulevard

Natchez, MS 39120
601-446-6502

Mississippi Department of Archives and History
P.O. Box 571
Jackson, MS 39205-0571
601-359-6876

Natchez Trace Parkway Library
R.R. 1, NT 143
Tupelo, MS 38801

Missouri
Mid-Continent Public Library
15616 East Highway 24
Independence, MO 64050
816-252-0950

University of Missouri
Kansas City General Library
5100 Rockhill Road
Kansas City, MO 64110

Montana
Historical Society of Montana Library and Archives
225 North Roberts Street
Helena, MT 59601

Museum of the Plains Indian Library and Archives
Highway 89, P.O. Box 400
Browning, MT 59417
406-338-2230

White Swan Memorial Library
Little Bighorn Battlefield National Monument
P.O. Box 39
Crow Agency, MT 59022
406-638-2621

University of Montana School of Law Library
Missoula, MT 59801

Nebraska
Center for Great Plains Studies
University of Nebraska
1213 Oldfather Hall
Lincoln, NE 68588-0314

Nebraska State Historical Society Library and
  Archives
1500 R Street
Lincoln, NE 68501
402-471-4771

Nevada
College Career and Vocational Resource Library
Nevada Urban Indians
401 West 2nd Street
Reno, NV 89503
702-329-2573

New Mexico
Albuquerque Public Library
Special Collections Branch
523 Central Avenue NE
Albuquerque, NM 87102

American Indian Law Center Library
University of New Mexico School of Law
1117 Stanford Street NE
Albuquerque, NM 87196
505-277-5462

Institute of American Indian Arts Library and Video
  Archives
P.O. Box 20007
Alexis Hall, St. Michael's Drive
Santa Fe, NM 87504
505-988-6423

Navajo Nation Library System
Book Distribution Services
P.O. Box 1484

Gallup, NM 87301
505-863-6058

New Mexico State Library
325 Don Gaspar Street
Santa Fe, NM 87503
505-827-3800

Zuni Archaeology Program Library
P.O. Box 339
Zuni, NM 87327
505-782-4814

New York
Akwesasne Library and Cultural Center
St. Regis Mohawk Reservation
Hogansburg, NY 13655
518-358-2240

American Museum of Natural History Library
Central Park West at 79th Street
New York, NY 10024
212-769-5400

New York Genealogical and Biographical Society
   Library
122 East 58th Street
New York, NY 10022-1939
212-755-8532

New York Public Library
Local History & Genealogy Division
Fifth Avenue and 42nd Street
New York, NY 10018
212-930-0828

North Carolina
Museum of the Cherokee Indian Library
P.O. Box 770-A, U.S. Hwy. 441 North
Cherokee, NC 28719
704-497-3481

Native American Library
Lumbee Regional Development Association
P.O. Box 637
Pembroke, NC 28372

Native American Resource Center Library
Pembroke State University
College Road
Pembroke, NC 28372
919-521-4214

North Carolina State Library
Genealogy & Archives Branch
109 East Jones Street
Raleigh, NC 27601-2807
919-733-7222

Schiele Museum Reference Library
Center for Southeastern Native Studies
P.O. Box 953, 1500 East Garrison Boulevard
Gastonia, NC 28053-0953
704-866-6900

North Dakota
State Historical Society of North Dakota Library and
    Heritage Center
Capitol Grounds
Bismarck, ND 58505
701-224-2666

Ohio
Ohio Historical Society
Archives & Library Division
1982 Velma Avenue
Columbus, OH 43211
614-297-2510

Mound City Group National Monument Library
16062 State Route 104
Chillicothe, OH 45601
614-774-1125

Rutherford B. Hayes Presidential Center Library
Spiegel Grove
Fremont, OH 43420
419-332-2081

Oklahoma
Cherokee Heritage Center Library
P.O. Box 515
Tahlequah, OK 74464

Institute of the Great Plains Library and Archives
601 Ferris
Elmer Thomas Park, P.O. Box 68
Lawton, OK 73502
405-353-5675

Oklahoma Historical Society
Indian Archives Division
2100 North Lincoln Boulevard
Oklahoma City, OK 73105
405-521-2481

Oklahoma State University Library
Stillwater, OK 74074

Western History Collection
Division of Manuscripts & Library
University of Oklahoma
401 West Brooks Street
Norman, OK 73069

Will Rogers Memorial Library
P.O. Box 157
Claremore, OK 74018
918-341-0719

Pennsylvania
American Indian Education Policy Center Library
Pennsylvania State University
320 Rackley Building
University Park, PA 16803
814-865-1489

**Council of Three Rivers American Indian Center
  Library**
200 Charles Street
Pittsburgh, PA 15238
412-782-4457

Library of American Indian Languages
American Philosophical Society
104 South Fifth Street
Philadelphia, PA 19106
215-627-0706

Rhode Island
Rhode Island Historical Society
121 Hope Street
Providence, RI 02906
401-331-8575

Tomaquag Indian Memorial Museum Library
Summit Road
Exeter, RI 02822
401-539-7795

South Carolina
South Carolina Department of Archives and History
1430 Senate Street
P.O. Box 11669
Columbia, SC 29211-1669
803-734-8596

South Dakota
American Indian Culture Research Center Library
Blue Cloud Abbey
P.O. Box 98
Marvin, SD 57251
605-432-5528

South Dakota Historical Resource Center
Memorial Building
Pierre, SD 57501

Tennessee
Chucalissa Archaeological Museum Library
1987 Indian Village Drive
Memphis, TN 38109
901-785-3160

Pinson Mounds State Archaeological Area Library
Rte. 1, Box 316
Ozier Road
Pinson, TN 38366
901-988-5614

Red Clay State Historical Park Library
Rte. 6, Box 733
Cleveland, TN 37311
615-472-2626

Tennessee State Library and Archives
403 7th Avenue N
Nashville, TN 37219
615-741-2764

Texas
Amon Carter Museum Photographic Archives
3501 Camp Bowie Boulevard
Ft. Worth, TX 76107-2631
817-738-1933

Dallas Public Library
Genealogy Section
1515 Young Street
Dallas, TX 75201

Houston Public Library
5300 Caroline Street
Houston, TX 77004

Panhandle–Plains Historical Museum Library and Archives
2401 Fourth Avenue
Canyon, TX 79016
806-655-7194

Utah
Family History Library
The Church of Jesus Christ of Latter-day Saints
35 NW Temple Street
Salt Lake City, UT 84150
801-240-2331

Ute Tribal Museum Library
Highway 40
P.O. Box 190
Fort Duchesne, UT 84026
801-722-4992

Virginia
Virginia State Library and Archives
Genealogy Department
11th Street at Capitol Square
Richmond, VA 23219–3491
804-786-2306

Washington
Oregon Province Archives
Crosby Library, Gonzaga University
Spokane, WA 99258
509-328-4220

Suquamish Tribal Archives and Museum Library
15838 Sandy Hook NE
Box 498
Suquamish, WA 98392
206-598-3311

University of Washington Libraries
Special Collections and Preservation Division
Allen Library
Seattle, WA 98195
206-543-1929

Washington State Historical Society Special
    Collections
315 North Stadium Way

Tacoma, WA 98403
206-593-2830

Yakima Nation Library
P.O. Box 151
Toppenish, WA 98948
509-865-2800

West Virginia
West Virginia Archives and History Division
Department of Culture and History
Capitol Complex
Charleston, WV 25305
304-348-0230

Wisconsin
Milwaukee Public Museum Library
800 West Wells Street
Milwaukee, WI 53233

State Historical Society of Wisconsin Library
816 State Street
Madison, WI 53706
608-264-6535

Stockbridge Munsee Historical Library
Route 1, Box 300
Bowler, WI 54416

Wyoming
Harold McCracken Research Library
Buffalo Bill Historical Center
720 Sheridan Avenue
Cody, WY 82414
307-587-4771

COMPUTER GENEALOGY

Ancestral File Operations Unit
50 East North Temple Street
Salt Lake City, UT 84150
801-240-2584

Write or call for information on the Family History Library's Personal Ancestral File (PAF) software.

Pence, Richard A. *Computer Genealogy: A Guide to Research Through High Technology*. **Salt Lake City: Ancestry, Inc., 1991.**

A comprehensive introduction to the use of computers in genealogical research. Though now a bit outdated, the book provides good coverage of the basics and describes software programs that are still popular today.

Przecha, Donna, and Lowrey, Joan. *Guide to Genealogy Software*. **Baltimore: Genealogical Publishing Co., 1993.**

As computer software packages can be quite expensive, it is important to make a well-informed decision when choosing one. Przecha and Lowrey evaluate more than fifty computer programs of interest to genealogists.

INTERNET WEB SITES

Everton Publishers Genealogy Page
http://www.everton.com

This page contains information on getting started as well as specific information on ethnic, religious, and social groups. Includes an online edition of the genealogical magazine *Everton's Genealogical Helper* and provides links to archives, libraries, and other Internet resources.

Genealogy Home Page
ftp://ftp.cac.psu.edu/pub/genealogy
http://ftp.cac.psu.edu/~saw/genealogy.html

By filling out the survey linked to this home page, you will be granted access to many genealogical links, allowing you to communicate with other genealogists, search new databases, and find out about other genealogical software online.

LDS Research Guides
ftp://hipp.etsu.edu/pub/genealogy

This site focuses on the Research Outline Guides produced by the Family History Library in Salt Lake City. Subjects include getting started, frequently asked genealogy questions, and techniques for photograph dating.

National Archives and Records Administration
gopher://gopher.nara.gov
http://www.nara.gov

NARA is the government agency responsible for managing the records of the federal government. Through this page you can find the location and business hours for regional archives or access information on finding and using particular government documents.

U.S. Census Bureau
ftp://gateway.census.gov
http://www.census.gov

From this site you can access statistics about population, housing, economy, and geography as compiled by the U.S. Department of Commerce Bureau of the Census. You can also do specific word searches according to subject or geographic location.

World Wide Web Genealogy Demo Page
http://demo.genweb.org/gene/genedemo.html

This page is still under construction, but its goal is to "create a coordinated, interlinked, distributed worldwide genealogy database." Even in its incomplete form, GenWeb allows you to access all known genealogical databases searchable through the www.

Since the 1700s North American Indians have fought the displacement from their tribal lands. Often, displacement resulted from treaties between the United States and Indian tribes. In 1986, demonstrators protested outside the Bureau of Indian Affairs office in New York City against the relocation of Native Americans in northern Arizona.

Chapter 7
Native American Records and Documents

A number of government documents are concerned with Indian affairs. State and federal records that might help your research include Indian removal materials, land sales and leases, Indian fishing and hunting rights records, military records, Works Progress Administration records, and Civilian Conservation Corps, Indian Division records. The booklet "Government Depository Libraries" gives details and locations of universities and public libraries receiving government documents.

Indian Treaties

Indian treaties established land titles and rights and serve as early legal documents for genealogical records and family and tribal histories. The first in a long series of treaties began with the Delaware Tribe on September 17, 1778, and was signed at Fort Pitt. By 1871 most of the Indian tribes and bands in the United States had signed more than 382 treaties and agreements ceding most or all of their ancestral lands in exchange for reservations and government assistance. This is a detailed record of the dispossession and decline of an indigenous people, at whose expense endless waves of new immigrants arrived to settle and expand.

Seven of the early Cherokee treaties were signed by two of my distant ancestors, John McLemore (Euskulacau/ Euquellooka) and his brother Robin McLemore. From places like Firey Gizzard and Battle Creek in Old Nation McLemores' Cove, and Going Snake District, in the shadows of Lookout and Pigeon Mountains (in what is now Georgia and Tennessee) and from Wills Town and other old native settlement areas (in what is now Alabama), many

Cherokee and Creek people gathered at the concentration camp at Ross's Landing near Chattanooga in the 1830s before walking the Trail of Tears.

Now we are drawn back into these treaties for many reasons, especially for the gathering of historical names. Here we find musical, descriptive names of headmen and medicine men. The names, like the persons who earned them, resonate with the respected traditions of diverse cultures. Path Killer (Nenohuttahe), Sour Mush (John Greenwood), and Turtle at Home (Sullicookiewalar) were some of the principal Cherokee treaty signers whose names appear on a number of treaties. Night Thunder (Ne-be-coim) of the Pillager Band of Chippewa and some of the Sioux signatures seem to echo their spiritual closeness to nature, like He Moves the Ghosts or Shadows (Na-ghee-yoo-shkan), White Dog (Shoank'-a-ska), Sacred Light or Medicine Bottle (Wa-kan-o-zhan), Walker on the Medicine Stones or Boulders (Too-kan-a-hena-ma-nee), and Many Lightnings (Wa-kan-hendee-o-ta).

An incredible amount of our heritage lives in this collection of documented change, from the first treaty with the Delaware in 1778 to the last agreement with the Columbia and Colville in 1883, covering more than a century of our history. For a comprehensive listing of Indian treaties, consult *Indian Treaties* by Charles J. Kappler (Washington, DC: U.S. Government Printing Office, 1904). This reference volume is usually available only in university reference and law libraries. The treaties document a particularly turbulent period in our nation's history, as well as some of our personal tribal histories. These legal documents may be of only peripheral value to most genealogical work, but if you can find a copy, it is a valuable reference tool for the names of key tribal individuals who were signatories on the treaties, and whose lives were forever changed by them. If your ancestors belonged to a tribe that was affected by a treaty, you will want to read about the changes it caused. This research may help you to determine why your ancestors suddenly moved west or why their land became part of a reservation.

You will be able to connect events in your family history with larger events in Native American history.

The Bureau of Indian Affairs

Established in 1824 under the jurisdiction of the Department of War, the Bureau of Indian Affairs (BIA) was transferred in 1849 to the Department of the Interior. Today this bureaucracy maintains a series of regional offices responsible for the ongoing affairs of one or more tribes in each region. When dealing with federally recognized tribes, you need to know where to locate your records. If you are unsure where to begin, write to the BIA in Washington, DC, requesting the tribal genealogical forms.

The BIA has undergone significant changes over its more than sixteen years, and it has documented some major areas of U.S. tribal histories. You will find much here to explore, especially the old census lists and enrollment records. Indian Land Claims materials, identified by tribe and docket number, are held by the Indian Claims Commission, 1730 K Street NW, Washington, DC 20540.

Photographs and maps of Indian affairs at the BIA are another rich resource. Thousands of fascinating photographs are housed in the Audio-Visual Archives Division of the National Archives and Records Center.

Record Group #75 contains the historical materials of the BIA, and much of this is available on microfilm. Like many things in the capital, this system and the BIA have undergone periodic changes, so you will need to consult the various indexes to find your information.

Another valuable set of resources is the annual reports of the Commissioner of Indian Affairs and the Secretary of the Interior, which include additional information on all Indian tribes. Major public libraries should have these books on their shelves.

Records of Federally Unrecognized Tribes

Many tribes and bands of American Indians, especially those east of the Mississippi River, do not have federal recognition for a variety of complex reasons. During more than 100 years of government/tribal treatymaking, numerous tribes, villages, bands, and groups of Indian people were assigned to share common reservations with larger neighboring tribes. Many refused, or found conditions unacceptable. Today many tribes are requesting formal federal recognition; a number of them have been turned down, but will try again. Many of these tribes maintain tribal councils and offices. If you believe that your bloodlines descend from one or more of these groups, you will want to make contact with the tribal office.

In addition, many contemporary Native Americans are listing themselves on their business cards, brochures, and in literature as Non-Federally Recognized Indians (NFRI) for a variety of personal and political reasons. Some call themselves Non-Government Enrolled Indians (NGEI) or Non-Government Enrolled Descendants (NGED). This is partly a result of personal sensitivity and political protest of federal and tribal government regulations that closely define who is Indian, and who is not. All of this makes tribal genealogical work more arduous, yet it is important to be aware of the many sensitivities that surround tribal enrollment issues.

Resources

NATIVE AMERICAN GENEALOGY

American Indians: A Select Catalog of National Archives. **Microfilm Publications, National Archives Trust Fund Board, U.S. General Services Administrations: Washington, DC, 1984.**

> This comprehensive listing is divided into civilian and military records, yet is only a portion of manuscript materials relating to Native Americans in the National Archives.

Bell, George M., Sr. *Genealogy of Old and New Cherokee Indian Families*. **Bartlesville, OK: G. M. Bell, 1972.**

> Extensive and valuable data for research on Cherokee bloodlines.

Carpenter, Cecelia Svinth. *How to Research American Indian Blood Lines, Meico*. **South Prairie, WA: Associated Edition, 1984.**

> The author shares her own personal search as a Native American historian and researcher. She delves further into her Nisqually Indian lineage and personal family history, and then expertly guides the reader toward his or her own goals. A rich resource.

Kirkham, E. Kay. *Our Native Americans and Their Records of Genealogical Value*, **2 vols. Logan, UT: Everton Publishers, 1980, 1984.**

> Information on specific records, and how to access additional details. "Degree of Blood Explained," "A Glossary

of Indian Information" and "How to Use Indian Records" are some of the extremely helpful chapters.

Reed, Robert D. *How and Where to Research Your Ethnic-American Cultural Heritage: Native Americans.* **Saratoga, CA: Author, 1979.**

Pamphlet listing important resources and where to obtain them.

Smith, Jesse Carney. *Ethnic Genealogy: A Research Guide.* **Foreword by Alex Haley. Westport, CT: Greenwood Publishing Group, 1983.**

Valuable reference book, especially for those seeking American Indian ancestry. Comprehensive and user-friendly.

Wright, Norman E. *Preserving Your American Heritage.* **Provo, UT: Brigham Young University Press, 1981.**

Especially good coverage of Native American research.

Chapter 8
Preserving What You Find

"I sat in a schoolroom in this town and listened to a teacher say there were no more Pequots in Ledyard because none of them lived through the massacre. But there I was, and I was a Pequot, living on the reservation. I might have been living on another planet."
—Theresa Bell, Director, Mashantucket Pequot Museum, Ledyard, Connecticut, 1990

"I am the last full-blood Chunut left. My children are part Spanish. I am the only one who knows the whole Chunut or Wowol language. When I am gone no one will have it. I have to be the last."
—Yokut Woman (California)

You have set up a simple system to keep your growing numbers of records in order so you can go back, as you will want to do (repeatedly), to check facts, review, and add newfound facts, folklore, photos, and documents. Yours can be a brief project with a special goal, which may end once the goal is achieved. Researching your Native American roots might also grow on you; you may find it more compelling and hard to put away. However it is with you, follow your system carefully and preserve what you find. The pride you take in doing this work will be a fine reward, and your care and thoroughness will be greatly appreciated by family members with whom you share your research and by future family historians. For centuries, Native Americans have struggled to preserve and celebrate their heritage in the face by discrimination, attempts to assimilate their culture, and history books that ignored their valuable contributions. As a Native American family historian, you have the important responsibility of reclaiming your past and putting it into a form that opens it up to family members and others who want to share it.

Notebooks and Files

A big three-ring notebook, filled with lined loose-leaf paper with indexes, is an important tool for this project. Everything else can radiate from there, with files, oral histories, computer printouts, and whatever else you may add as you progress. A central notebook that you can easily carry on visits to libraries, relatives, and family reunions is your best asset for quick reference.

Index your notebook beginning with a first section consisting of a family overview, and your general ancestry chart(s), with perhaps some details of family history. The next eight sections might be each one of your eight major descent lines: the four great-grandparents on your father's side of the family, then the four great-grandparents on your mother's side of the family. Some of these might be blank in the beginning (or for some time), but set aside the space for them. The last section(s) of your notebook might be records of the sources, libraries, archives, cemeteries, or historical visits that you have found most helpful. By keeping your information on loose pages, you can easily add and subtract items and data as you progress. When you visit relatives, encourage them to write some personal family thoughts in your "Family Album."

You may want to make photocopies of old family photos to put in your various sections, so that family members can help you identify people and places in the photos. You may want to add the modern components of taped oral histories and video movies of family events. Your family history "documents" can include photocopies of pages from old Bibles, quilts, stitched samplers, old wedding dresses, and other personal family treasures that can be documented and saved.

Valuable documents like birth, marriage, and death certificates should be kept in safe files for easy reference. Some or all of these might be copied to put in your notebook, and to give to other family members who might want them. Social Security, health, and armed services records, along with other old family documents, should be kept in safe files. You can also list them in your notebook.

Make a file box for this project out of a sturdy cardboard box. Mark a manila folder for each of your eight major descent lines. You may want to have additional folders for correspondence, photos, and whatever else does not go readily into one of your family folders. In time you might need several boxes or file drawers, but in the beginning a three-ring notebook and file box should keep you and your project well-organized.

Family Group Sheets and Pedigree Charts

Standard forms developed by family historians and genealogists will help you organize your final results. You may decide to create your own personal forms and then make duplicate copies to use for all your work. Be sure to keep the vital data required for general genealogy or tribal membership status.

The family group sheet gathers the vital statistics for a single family: marriage details and names of children along with dates and places of birth, marriage, and death for each family member. If one or both of your parents have remarried, make a separate family group sheet for each remarriage and record the children and details from it.

Your pedigree chart shows the vital information from your family group sheets, stretching from you back to the earliest generations for which you have information. Some of these family pedigree sheets show four or five generations at a glance; then you use additional pedigree sheets for succeeding generations. You may want to make one long fold-out sheet that includes ten generations or more. This type of pedigree chart is excellent to take along when you do family research, because all your names are right there, and you can readily see the gaps where information needs to be found and filled in.

Some artists have drawn and painted vines, plants, or stylized trees into their finished family tree charts. You may want to make sketches of family members to go beside their names. If you are especially proud of your pedigree chart, have it framed for all to see.

Perhaps you prefer a professional-looking pedigree chart, which is the type to submit for tribal genealogy or any other professional work. The most important thing is to be clear and to record details carefully in their proper places.

Your Pedigree Chart

In a simple chart like this one you can show your immediate four generations, going back to your eight great-grandparents. This will give you the eight major family names from which you are descended.)

Great-grandfather_____
b. (born)_____
md. (married)_____
d. (died)_____

Grandfather_____
b._____
md._____
d._____

Great-grandmother_____
b._____
d._____

Grandmother_____
b._____
d._____

Father_____
b._____
md._____
d._____

You_____
b._____
md._____
d._____

Mother_____
b._____
d._____

Essays

Talking to relatives and listening to them recount various periods in your family's history may stimulate you to write your own family history, or portions of it. Collect the family stories and folklore. Perhaps there is a particular character you feel drawn to: a favorite uncle, or a distant grandmother, or a younger cousin whom you might want to write about and get to know better.

Were any of your early ancestors warriors, whalers, ironworkers, artists, herbalists, or healers? You may want to write specifically about a certain occupation and how it has been traditionally practiced by your family.

The books listed in the **Resources** may give you ideas for writing a biography or autobiography.

Family History Books

Has anyone written a book on your family? More and more personal books on family histories are being published each year. Many of them are self-published using desktop computer printing facilities. You might begin by preparing your best ten to twelve pages of family findings. Copy these, if you can, and send them, or give them, to family members who have helped you with this work—like a "family newsletter." Holidays and family reunions are bright opportunities for this kind of activity to attract enthusiasm. Perhaps an annual update will be possible. Sometimes this leads to creating a family book.

Resources

FAMILY GROUP SHEETS AND PEDIGREE CHARTS

Evelyn Spears Family Group Sheet Exchange
East 12502 Frideger
Elk, WA 99009

> A service that provides previously researched family group sheets from a catalog of about 14,000, at a charge of about ten dollars per surname requested.

Genealogical Center, Inc.
International Family Group Sheet Exchange
P.O. Box 17698
Tampa, FL 33682

> Request their catalog of over 8,000 surnames by mail. They charge thirty cents per page of researched data, and studies can range from ten to 300 pages.

Schreiner-Yantis Family Group Sheets
6818 Lois Drive
Springfield, VA 22150

> These family group sheets, pedigree charts, and other forms are widely considered the finest available. Write for a catalog and list of prices.

PREPARING A WRITTEN FAMILY HISTORY

Carroll, F. Michael. *Portrait of My Family*. Baltimore: Genealogical Publishing Co., 1990.

> This 140-page, illustrated activity book enables you to

fill in all of your details as you gain the data from your research, with plenty of space for additional information.

Cheney, Theodore A. Rees. *Writing Creative Non-fiction: How to Use Fiction Techniques to Make Your Nonfiction More Interesting, Dramatic and Vivid.* **Cincinnati, OH: Writer's Digest Books, 1987.**

This book will help you to make your written family history interesting as well as informative. Includes tricks of the writing trade to help your nonfiction read more like a novel.

Fletcher, William P. *Record Your Family History.* **Berkeley, CA: Ten Speed Press, 1989.**

An excellent guide to preserving your family history on audio and videotape. Includes sample questions, examples of what to listen for, and important interview techniques.

Jordan, Lewis. *Cite Your Sources: A Manual for Documenting Family Histories and Genealogical Records.* **Jackson: University Press of Mississippi, 1980.**

Citing your sources ensures accuracy in your genealogical project. This book gives advice on how to make citations clear for a variety of genealogical sources.

McLaughlin, Paul. *A Family Remembers.* **North Vancouver, BC: Self-Counsel Press, 1993.**

An excellent guide to creating a family memoir using tape recorders and video cameras.

Zinsser, William. *On Writing Well: An Informal Guide to Writing Nonfiction.* **New York: Harper & Row, 1985.**

A user-friendly, patient guide to writing and revising a solid work of nonfiction.

NATIVE AMERICAN BIOGRAPHY AND AUTOBIOGRAPHY

Abeita, Louise. *I Am a Pueblo Indian Girl*. **New York: William Morrow, 1939.**

Beautifully illustrated by American Indian artists, this autobiography describes a young girl's life with sensitive details and fine poetry.

Antell, Will. *William Wipple Warren: Ojibway Historian*. **Minneapolis: Dillon Press, 1972.**

This stunning biography details the life of the noted Ojibway author/historian, born in 1825, with fascinating background about his family and work in the Territorial House of Representatives during a pivotal time in American history.

Barrett, Steven Melvil, ed. *Geronimo: His Own Story*. **New York: E. P. Dutton, Ballantine Books, 1970.**

Geronimo, the Apache leader, gives a unique cultural and historical account of his people in this story of his life, which he dictated while imprisoned at Fort Sill, Oklahoma Territory.

Bennett, Kay. *Kaibah: Recollections of a Navajo Girlhood*. **Los Angeles: Western Lore Press, 1964.**

Love and understanding infuse this personal story of Navajo family life, as Kay Bennett writes of her girlhood years growing up on a reservation from 1928 to 1935.

Black Hawk. *Black Hawk: An Autobiography*. **Edited by Donald Jackson. Urbana: University of Illinois Press, 1955.**

Black Hawk, at seventy years of age, tells of his early battles with other tribes and of his last flight from the U.S. Army and the massacre of his people at Bad Axe, Wisconsin, in 1832. Black Hawk, the famous Sac (Sauk) Indian Chief, was immortalized by the Black Hawk War of 1832, which was considered the final battle for the Old Northwest.

Blackman, Margaret B. *During My Time: Florence Edenshaw Davidson, A Haida Woman*. Seattle: University of Washington Press, 1990.

This life history, the first one about the life of a Northwest Coast Indian woman, is a living link with cultural traditions as the Haida were undergoing changes that would forever alter their way of life.

Chief Joseph. *Chief Joseph's Own Story*. Billings: Montana Reading Publications, 1972.

In an oration he delivered in Washington, DC, in 1879, Chief Joseph traces the history of Nez Perce contact with non-Indians from 1779, when French trappers traveled into eastern Oregon, to the time of his surrender and exile to Oklahoma Territory.

Cohoe, William. *A Cheyenne Sketchbook*. Norman: University of Oklahoma Press, 1964.

Haunting, expressive accounts by the author/illustrator, one of seventy-two warriors from the Great Plains taken in 1875 as prisoners to Fort Marion, Florida, where he sketched these scenes from his past and from his life as a prisoner.

Crashing Thunder. *Crashing Thunder: The Autobiography of a Winnebago*. Edited by Paul Radin. New York: Dover Books, 1963.

This life story, first published in 1920, begins with the author's boyhood. Many Winnebago tribal customs are revealed in this lovely reprint.

Crow Dog, Mary, and Erdoes, Richard. *Lakota Woman*. New York: Harper Collins, 1991.

Mary Crow Dog, a Lakota mixed-blood activist, poignantly recalls her turbulent life as a young, troubled American Indian Movement member. She is the former wife of Lakota Medicine Man Leonard Crow Dog. She is also known as Mary Brave Bird. The description of the siege at Wounded Knee is especially haunting.

Eastman, Charles Alexander. *Indian Boyhood.* **New York: Dover Books, 1971.**

First-person account of the everyday life of the author as a young boy just before the reservation period. He beautifully interweaves his tribe's traditions and religious beliefs, recording a precious time in Sioux history.

Fitzgerald, Michael O. *Yellowtail, Crow Medicine Man and Sun Dance Chief: An Autobiography.* **Norman: University of Oklahoma Press, 1991.**

The author provides considerable insight into sacred spiritual dimensions of Crow Indian life.

Freuchen, Pipaluk. *Eskimo Boy.* **New York: Lothrop, Lee & Shepard, 1951.**

The story of Ivik, a young Eskimo boy, who vows to support his family after his father is killed in a hunting accident. Explores the traumas and travails of Eskimo boyhood and life.

Henry, Christopher E. *Ben Nighthorse Campbell: Cheyenne Chief—U.S. Senate.* **New York: Chelsea House, 1994.**

An account of how a contemporary statesman mixes native traditions with modern life in Washington, DC.

Holler, Anne. *Pocahontas: Powhatan Peacemaker.* **New York: Chelsea House, 1993.**

The brief but historically important life of this young Algonquian woman is sensitively chronicled. Some misconceptions are dispelled.

Howard, Harold P. *Sacajawea.* **Norman: University of Oklahoma Press, 1977.**

Read about the life of Lewis and Clark's famous Shoshoni guide, Sacajawea, whose help was pivotal to the exploration of American land in the early 1800s.

Josie, Edith. *Here Are the News*. Toronto, Ontario: Clark, Irwin & Co., 1966.

Edith Josie wrote a newspaper column for the *Whitehorse Star,* reporting on life in the Native American village of Old Crow, on the banks of the Porcupine River north of the Arctic Circle.

Krupat, Arnold, ed. *Native American Autobiography: An Anthology*. Madison: University of Wisconsin Press, 1994.

Examines the lives, the literature, and the history of select American Indian authors.

La Pointe, Frank. *The Sioux Today*. New York: Macmillan, 1972.

Personal vignettes of the lives of contemporary Sioux people, based on the author's own reservation experiences, dispel various stereotypes.

Lyons, Oren. *Dog Story*. New York: Holiday House, 1973.

Illustrated by the author, this book recounts his early boyhood on the Onondaga Reservation in upstate New York, and the closeness that developed between him and his dog.

MacDonald, Peter. *The Last Warrior: Peter MacDonald and the Navajo Nation*. Library of the American Indian. New York: Crown Publishing Group, 1993.

Personal odyssey of this famous and embattled former Navajo leader.

Mankiller, Wilma Pearl, and Wallis, Michael. *Mankiller: A Chief and Her People*. New York: St. Martin's Press, 1993.

The first woman to become Principal Chief of the Cherokee Nation in Oklahoma shares her amazing life and spirit of achievement.

Marquis, Thomas B. *Wooden Leg: A Warrior Who Fought Custer*. Lincoln: University of Nebraska Press, 1962.

Reprint of the 1931 narrative recalling the fight against General George Armstrong Custer at the Battle of the Little Bighorn, and commenting on Cheyenne daily life and tribal customs.

Momaday, N. Scott. *The Names*. Tempe: University of Arizona Press, 1987.

The author's poignant description of his boyhood, interwoven with his research of family history and quest for his tribal history.

Mourning Dove. *Mourning Dove: A Salishan Autobiography*. Edited by Jay Miller. Lincoln: University of Nebraska Press, 1990.

A moving tribute to this fascinating woman and her life; the book was assembled from the many notes of this talented native scholar.

Neihardt, John, and Black Elk. *Black Elk Speaks: Being the Life of a Holy Man of the Oglala Sioux*. Lincoln: University of Nebraska Press, 1961.

This moving personal narrative, first published in 1932, by one of the great spiritual leaders of the Oglala Sioux, recounts his life from early boyhood (he was born in 1863), to the massacre at Wounded Knee in 1890 and the gathering of the Oglala Sioux on the Pine Ridge Reservation in South Dakota.

Plenty-Coups. *Plenty-Coups, Chief of the Crows*. Edited by Frank Bird Linderman. Lincoln: University of Nebraska Press, 1962.

Chief Plenty-Coups, in his eighties, reflects upon his boyhood and how he became a chief, describing tribal customs of the Crow Indians.

Qoyawayma, Polingaysi [Elizabeth Q. White]. *No Turning Back: A Hopi Indian Woman's Struggle to Live in Two Worlds.* **Albuquerque: University of New Mexico Press, 1964.**

Born at Old Oraibi, Arizona in c.1892, this noted writer, teacher, potter, and musician was awarded the U.S. Distinguished Service Award for her long career in Indian education. This is the story of her attempt to bridge the gap between the world of her people and the world of non-Indians.

Senungetuk, Joseph E. *Give or Take a Century: An Eskimo Chronicle.* **San Francisco: Indian Historian Press, 1970.**

The history of the author's Eskimo family and their traditions.

Seymour, Tryntje Van Ness. *The Gift of Changing Woman.* **New York: Henry Holt & Co., 1993.**

Changing Woman, the legendary ancestor of all the Apache, brings her power to an Apache girl coming of age in a special ceremony that celebrates life, the cycles of nature, and respect for the natural world.

Talayesva, Don C. *Sun Chief: The Autobiography of a Hopi Indian.* **Edited by Leo W. Simmons. New Haven, CT: Yale University Press, 1942, 1972.**

Surveys, over a span of fifty years, the life of a Hopi Indian in Oraibi, Arizona.

Two Leggings. *Two Leggings: The Making of a Crow Warrior.* **Edited by Peter Nabakov. New York: Crowell, 1967.**

This autobiography details the author's everyday life, giving a great deal of information on the religious and social values of the Plains Indian people.

Wallace, Paul. *White Roots of Peace: Iroquois Book of Life.* **Foreword by Chief Leon Shenandoah and epilogue by John Mohawk. Sante Fe: Clear Light Publishers, 1980.**

The extraordinary story of a charismatic spiritual leader whose vision and political genius brought order and peace to the Iroquois in a time of chaos.

Waters, Frank. *Brave Are My People: Indian Heroes Not Forgotten.* **Santa Fe: Clear Light Publishers, 1993.**

Biographies of Native American prophets, warriors, statesmen, and orators told by the noted author of more than twenty books, who has been nominated five times for the Nobel Prize in Literature.

Yagoda, Ben. *Will Rogers: A Biography.* **New York: Knopf, 1993.**

Biography of the noted Cherokee humorist, entertainer, gifted commentator, and writer, who lived from 1879 to 1935.

Glossary

Aleut   People of the Aleutian Islands, which stretches almost 1,200 miles west of the tip of Alaska into the Pacific Ocean.

American Indian   People native (indigenous) to the Americas, especially the United States.

assimilation (acculturation)   A policy and effort to absorb Native American people into mainstream white culture.

band   An extended family or subdivision of an Indian tribe.

BIA (Bureau of Indian Affairs)   Federal agency formed in 1824 to handle Indian issues and manage Indian lands and monies.

bloodlines   The lines of descent; pedigree; family and ethnic heritage.

confederacy   Political union of several or many tribes.

cosmology   Theory explaining the nature (origin) of the universe.

culture area   A classification to understand various tribes living in a geographical area and sharing similar lifeways.

descent (in lineage)   The passing from one ancestor to another.

displacement   Ousting (removing) a people from their natural habitat.

ethnobotany   The study of how a culture uses its floral environments.

ethnology   The study of cultures, especially their historic developments.

geopolitical   Combination of geographical and political factors.

Indian   Pertaining to North American Indians; native

people indigenous to the Americas, also known as
Native Americans.

Indian Removal Act (1830) Federal relocation of eastern
Indians to Indian Territory west of the Mississippi
River.

Indian Reorganization Act (1934) Provided for restoration of tribal governments.

Indian reservation Area set aside by the government for
Native Americans.

Indian territory Originally eastern Oklahoma, about
31,000 square miles, set aside for the displaced eastern tribes.

Indian treaties More than 382 agreements between Indians and the federal government (or states) ceding
most of their ancestral lands for reservations, between
1778 and 1871.

matriarchy Society governed by females, with descent
reckoned in the female line.

Native Americans People indigenous to the Americas.

oral tradition History passed down orally, especially
through stories.

patriarchy Society governed by males, with descent traced
through the male line.

phratry Group of clans within a tribe.

powwow Native American social gathering or ceremony.

prehistoric The period of time before written history.

relocation Forced removal of a tribe or people from one
location to another.

termination Federal policy in the 1950s attempting to
end the special protective relationship between the
U.S. government and Indians.

tribe Indian social/political organization with shared descent, culture, and territory.

trust lands Special protected lands, not true reservations.

Index

ABOUT THE AUTHOR

E. Barrie Kavasch is of Creek, Cherokee, and Powhatan descent and has traced her ancestry directly back fourteen generations to Chief Powhatan through his noted daughter, Pocahontas. She is the author of *Native Harvests* and *Enduring Harvests: Native American Foods and Festivals for Every Season.*

ILLUSTRATION CREDITS

Cover, J. J. Foxx/NYC from the Abrams book *The Turquoise Trail.* Cover inset, Smithsonian Institution Photo No. 3391-B. Pp. 2, 4, 6, 9, 17, 27, 40, 47, 52, 55, 61, 79, 82, 87, 109, 113, 115, 142, BETTMANN. *Color insert:* pp. 2, 3, 4, 5, 10, 11, 14, BETTMANN; p. 6, © J. J. Foxx/NYC; p. 7, © Steven Kosek; pp. 8, 9, © E. Barrie Kavasch; pp. 12, 13, 15, 16, AP/Wide World Photos.

LAYOUT AND DESIGN

Kim Sonsky